Beyond the Sallagh Braes

A memoir of a Northern Irish woman
and her travels.

Morna Croft

Copyright © Morna Croft, 2021
Published: 2021 by The Book Reality Experience

ISBN: 978-0-6489497-2-5 Paperback Edition
ISBN: 978-0-6450629-4-6 EBook Edition

***

This book is a memoir, reflecting the author's present recollections of experiences over time. This means that some details may vary from fact. Some names and characteristics have been changed, some events have been compressed, and some dialogue has been recreated. Memory can be a fickle thing, so the Author trusts that any minor errors in times, dates and details of particular events will be understood.

Some names and identifying details have been changed to protect the privacy of individuals.

Cover Design by Luke Buxton | www.lukebuxton.com

To

My beloved husband
without whose help this book would
never have come into being.

The Farm In The Antrim Hills

"A drawer mummy?"

It must have been the year 1960 because she was carefully placing my baby sister in the big Pedigree pram. I know it was before I started primary school and I watched her and waited for her to answer.

"Your daddy and I were living with your grandmother when we brought you home from the hospital. It was unlucky to bring the cot or the pram home before the baby." I must have looked puzzled because she said, "Your grandmother took the bottom drawer from her big chest of drawers and she put a pillow in it and we made up a little bed for you. Your daddy brought this pram home for you a couple of days later."

I had been too young to question when we had moved to the farm, situated in the Antrim Hills above Larne.

My father worked the land as his father before him. There had been a lot of hard work involved in taking it from a boggy hillside with rushes to lush hay-making meadows. My father worked that land with the sweat of his brow, but that wasn't all he did. He had a fulltime job as a salesman in a furniture shop in the nearby town as well.

Back on the farm, the hay was cut with a scythe and arranged into rows with a wooden rake. The rows were turned to dry in the sun when the weather was good. There was no question of the weather not being good, he listened to the weather forecast on the old wireless to make sure the sun would shine for a few days before mowing it. We couldn't afford to lose the hay as we needed it to feed the animals in winter. Once dry, it was built into small hay rucks and later transferred into large hay pikes, as they were known in our part of the country.

The walls, we called them ditches, separating the fields were built from the stone that was plentiful on the hillside, and if they fell into disrepair my father rebuilt them by hand. My mother worked alongside him — she worked like a man. The dent on her wedding ring was from lifting the stones for him to build the stone ditches. My father wanted to keep sheep and in order to do so he had to erect fences with paling posts and barbed wire in some areas. My mother helped him with those as well, I remember her blinking every time the sledge hammer hit the post she was holding steady for him. Like every farmer's wife, she also had the meals to prepare while the men sat at the table or in the hay field and talked.

They were a good looking couple, my mother and father, not that I am biased of course. My father was tall, dark haired and muscular because of the hard work I suppose. He had a handsome face and a ready smile.

My mother was teased by some of the old farmers because she had won a couple of local beauty contests before she was married. I loved it if she wore her lipstick when she collected me from school. I used to tell her she was the nicest looking mummy at the school. She would laugh, and tossing back her head of brown curls she would say, "Do you think so?"

Although it was a farm with a lot of acres, the house was of a modest size and built of stone, as were the outbuildings. A stream ran through the land and we always had fresh spring water. There was no electricity, so the evening light was supplied by paraffin oil lamps and candles. Cooking was done mostly on the wood burning stove or the gas cooker, which was used first thing in the morning if the stove had gone out.

There was no such thing as central heating in the house. Our clothes were warmed by the fire before dressing for school and a big pot of porridge bubbled beside the singing kettle on top of the stove. We had our own milk and eggs and my mother was a great baker, so we were not short of anything. I can still remember the oven soda bread with raisins, wheaten bread, griddle sodas, potato farls and the pancakes. I had three brothers and three sisters and we loved it if she was baking when we came home from school. Sometimes she would have a big pot of custard or rice pudding on top of the stove and that was even more popular than the bread.

Our lane was long and rough and the white sliced bread brought by the baker was left at the neighbouring farm. It gave my mother a reason to visit and have a cup of tea and a chat with the farmer's wife. Looking after a big family and doing the farm work meant this was the only chance she had to talk to another woman.

My brother and I loved it if she took us with her for company as we got to play with the children. It was exciting walking home in the moonlight or when there was frost or snow. It turned the landscape into a magical world. They say people know where they were or what they were doing when they heard that President John F. Kennedy had been shot in 1963. We were at the neighbour's house when it was announced on the wireless and it came as a great shock to all of us.

The bread was delivered around the country in a baker's van. We loved it when Dan the baker came and we knew there would be sugary Paris buns or an apple tart along with a couple of sliced pan loaves for making toast. That wasn't all the baker delivered, we got the weekly newspaper and comics, the *Dandy* and the *Beano*. When I was a little older I got *Jackie* magazine with posters of the Beatles and other pop groups. I can still see those posters on the pale green distempered walls of my bedroom.

Paddy the butcher came in his little van on a Saturday night. My mother bought steak for my father and minced steak and sausages for the rest of us. Now, Paddy had a charm for the removal of warts. He gave you an old penny if you had a wart but you were not allowed to thank him for it. If you did the charm wouldn't work and you would be stuck with the wart forever. If you did as you were told the wart would disappear, where it went to we never found out.

A big blue grocery van came every Friday, you could go inside it and choose what you wanted. My mother always bought a few groceries and she always bought packets of Fruit Pastilles for us to share. We didn't get a lot of groceries from the van because my father took a list to a shop in the town, near to his work. The groceries were packed into cardboard boxes and he collected them on his way home. I remember him calling the groceries the rations, I thought it strange at the time but I later found out that although the Second World War ended in 1945 rationing didn't end until 1954. I suppose he used the term out of habit.

The coal lorry delivered a ton of coal to the farm and my mother would say to a couple of the children, "Go out and play but count the bags that are taken off the lorry."

The oil man used to bring paraffin oil for the room heater and the lamps, not only did we have oil lamps in the house but hurricane lamps for outside. My father used them for checking the stock were alright when he came home from work on a winter's night. They gave light while he helped a cow to calf or a sheep to lamb.

Apart from these deliveries and family calling, we had three more regular visitors. They were all farmers who lived alone and within walking distance of our farm. As a child I thought they were ancient but they were probably in their early seventies. They never seemed to visit at the same time as each other, but whether that was by design or accident I don't know. Each one had different character traits.

James had a flat cap, hanging lip and a pair of glasses, my mother threatened to marry me off to him if I didn't behave myself. He was the type of man who would have sat all night when he came to visit. He had to be given the hint to go home as my father had to go to work the next day.

Willie had a worse habit of sitting so close to the fire that the smell of his working clothes was terrible in the heat.

Harry was a tall thin man and he had a constant drip at his nose in winter. He was a kindly soul and my mother was fond of him. They would have a bit of banter together and knowing he was a staunch Roman Catholic my mother would ask him if she could borrow his step ladder to put up the Union Jack for the Twelfth of July. He said, "Only if you walk with me on the Fifteenth of August." He knew she was only joking and the two of them would have a good laugh.

My father thought the men were lonely and they visited for the company and whatever news they could hear. My mother though they liked having a cup of tea made for them and some of her home baked bread. They were probably both right.

Our days out were rare, they were mainly used for visiting family. Occasionally we went for a drive up the coast for an ice-cream. With two adults in the front seats of the car the seven children had to pile into the back seat. The big ones held the wee ones on their laps and my mother shouted every two minutes, "Don't lean against the doors." She must have been worried her precious cargo would spill out if the doors burst open.

All in all I think it would be fair to say we were a happy family, and in no doubt about the love my parents had for each other and for us.

We didn't attend church very much in the early days but my parents instilled decency into us. We were taught right from wrong. My mother taught us our prayers and she sat and listened to us say them every night at bedtime. As we grew older the last thing we heard at night was my mother or father calling, "Don't forget to say your prayers." It was a bit like the television programme *The Walton's* in our house! Later when we lived nearer to the church we would walk to Sunday School. When we had to read in Church, woe betide us if we didn't read loudly enough for my father to hear.

Family holidays were out of the question; it would have been impossible to leave the farm, but what you never had, you never miss. The neighbourhood children were all the same. If you were lucky you went to stay with your granny for your holidays. I loved those holidays with my grandmother. I was a country child and it was lovely to see the sea.

Her little cottage was in the Sallagh Braes with a lovely view of the sea. The colour of the water changed all the time. Sometimes, it was grey like the sky. I loved it best when the sun was shining and it was blue and silver. Blue was my favourite colour.

My grandmother didn't drive, but she told me one day we would go to the beach, we would paddle in the sea and build sandcastles.

The little cottage sits empty now, abandoned of its people — filled with my memories.

Looking back, I suppose it was a typical Irish cottage, whitewashed with a Bangor Blue slated roof. The window frames and door were painted green. There were two large, flat topped stones, one on either side of the door. My grandmother had carried the limestone in bags from the local quarry to make the yard which was entered by a farm gate.

Inside it had only two rooms. One served as a bedroom and the other was a sitting room and kitchen. I remember it so well; there were handmade Irish lace curtains on the sash windows, and near one of the windows, a stand with a bird cage and a little budgie. When I sat on the settee with its flowery covers, I often got a shower of bird seed around me.

An Ale Plant sat near the window sill — a weird looking thing like a cauliflower in a glass sweetie jar. Every week it was topped up with sugar and water. It produced a sweet liquid, but whether it tasted like ale, I have no idea for children were not allowed to have any.

The kettle was always on the boil on the Rayburn stove. I can still feel the heat from it and all the cooking. I remember gathering mushrooms with my grandmother, bringing them home and roasting them on the Rayburn with a little butter. They were delicious.

A table, chairs and a food cupboard completed the furnishings. Life was simple then.

Water was carried in buckets from a spout of spring water up the road. I was washed standing up in one of the old-fashioned bread crocks.

The little cottage was seldom without visitors; they came for the warmth of my grandmother's friendship and they never left without having a cup of tea. Besides, my grandmother could sometimes be coaxed to take the cards from the pocket of her overall to tell them what the future held. You see, she had *The Gift*, but she only read for friends and family and only if she was in the notion of doing it. She gave hope to many — hope of better times to come. This was not something she charged for; just like her love and her laughter, it was freely given.

Something happened one night that was to remain etched in my memory forever.

The adults in the cottage were excited by something outside in the dark. Someone took my hand and drew me outside. The sky, which was usually black and starry, was lit up with the most amazing mass of moving green light. Even my sea was green! I could sense fear in the adults and I asked, "What is it?"

"It is the Northern Lights," I was quietly told. This was the Aurora Borealis, I would learn later as a primary school child.

Would I be afraid of this change in my lovely sea view now? Of course not; I would stand transfixed and enjoy the beauty of it. I suppose when something has been explained to us we quite often lose the fear of it.

Those holidays were something I looked forward to, a time when my grandmother would spoil me and give me her undivided attention. I would curl up beside her in her soft feather bed and she would give me a Murray Mint, take one herself and read me a story from the children's page in her magazine, *The People's Friend*.

There were seven children in our family; we were like steps of stairs. The only difference in us and the other children in the neighbourhood was our religion. We were Protestants in a mainly Catholic area. I remember getting a cuff on the ear one day because I asked a neighbour who he was going to vote for in the election. I also remember we had to stand in the cold porch of the two-classroom Catholic school while the other children said their prayers in the mornings.

My mother only played the Protestant card once. I had been put out into the little shed beside the school in winter to do my work because I had been caught talking in class. Someone told my mother they saw me sitting there with the hailstones blowing in on me and she was angry. She went down to the school and talked to the head mistress. She said, "I hope it is not because we are a different religion." The teacher was sent for and I was told to go back to class. When the teacher came back into the class a little later, her face was red and she looked cross. She walked over to me and pulled the hair at the back of my neck, under my pony tail. She jumped back when the hook on my blouse caught under her nail. "Get on with your work, Miss" was all she said.

The priest was lovely to me. He gave me a little hanky when the others were getting their rosary beads, but of course, being a child, I complained to my mother that I would rather have had the rosary beads.

My young brother started the school at age three — to make up the numbers, so it wouldn't have to close. I loved that wee school but not the outside toilet, which was a little tin hut. It was a dry toilet and nowadays when I see people having them on campsites to be eco-friendly, I don't envy them in any way. I attended that school until I was in primary six. I had been working very hard and studying for my eleven plus exam, which was a selection process for grammar school. The headmistress said I had a fair chance of passing with good marks. At that point, my parents decided to move to the town. They saw it as a step up in the world and an easier life. My father had lost a lot of sheep in the year of the big snow. The farm was put on the market and a date set for the auction.

We talked and recalled our memories of living on the farm and what we would miss. I thought of the meadow where I had picked pink ragged robin flowers and looked at the cuckoo spit on little lilac flowers. My mother had showed us how to make daisy chains and as little girls we adorned our hair with them. We had collected frog spawn every year and took jam jars of it into school for the nature table. We had such fun around the hay rucks and had picnics when my mother brought the tea to the field.

There was one day when I cut the inside of my upper arm on the surrounding barbed wire fence. I had a new collie pup on a lead and I was fearful it would get hurt and I forgot about myself. Thirteen stitches later, I vowed I would be more careful in the future. I remember my mother giving the doctor half a dozen duck eggs when he finished his work.

There was the little wooden hen house where I had caught my brothers smoking. I told my mother about them; I was three years older and it was expected that I should look after them.

I remembered my mother playing a joke one Easter. She got up early and replaced the eggs with chocolate ones in silver paper. My brother was so excited when he thought the ducks and hens had laid them especially for Easter. My brothers had been playing in the shed where the hay was stored and one of them cut his head when it connected with a sharp stone. I had to run to the next farm to ask the farmer if he would drive to the nearest phone on his tractor and phone the doctor. The doctor came and my mother held my brother's head while he stitched it. She was pleased when he told her she would have made a fine nurse. My mother presented him with another half dozen duck eggs when he was leaving.

At the back of the house was the byre where a cow kicked my mother and spilled the bucket of milk while she was milking, one morning. She came into the house crying, but she was more annoyed about the milk she needed for our breakfast than she was about herself. We had black tea with our bread and jam that day.

The far field was where the neighbour's bull chased me. My father was cutting thistles with a scythe when the bull came into our field. I had a little red tartan skirt and strapless sandals on, I ran like lightning and it gave chase. My sandals fell off and I ended up with jags in my poor feet. My mother managed to catch me as I fell over the wall just ahead of the ring on the bull's nose. My father put the hook of his stick through the ring and led the bull across the field. I was crying, but I thought my daddy was the bravest man in the world. He was my hero.

He could be cross sometimes, like the time when my brother and I left our positions when a bull was being moved from one field to another. It was being taken through the yard and we had been warned not to let it into the meadow as the hay was ready for cutting. When the bull headed towards us we stepped aside as we were so afraid. By the time my father had moved him to the right field he was tired enough to have calmed down.

As children, we didn't really understand that the move to the town would mean the loss of our freedom. Instead of acres of land to play in we would have a small back garden. My mother and father having been used to the country all their lives, wouldn't be keen for us to be out of their sight in the town.

There had been a buzz in the neighbourhood about the farm being up for sale and the day of the auction saw a good turnout. Most of the men there couldn't have afforded it, but curiosity is a wonderful thing in farming communities and it was a day off for most of them after seeing to their animals.

My mother kept us all in the house and we were hushed to keep quiet. She had a vested interest in hearing how the proceedings went. Part way through the auction my father and the auctioneer came into the house to decide whether the latest bid should be accepted. The highest bidder was a neighbouring farmer and in the country way of saying things, "the ground lay into his." This was probably the reason the other farmers weren't bidding against him, although they looked surprised that he was bidding at all. However, my father thought the bid was reasonable and he let the farm go. We later discovered that the farmer was bidding for someone else and not himself after all. My father just said, "Ugh, these are the things you are up against."

I don't remember much about the weeks that followed or indeed the move, but I do remember the first night in the new three-bedroom house. My mother never slept a wink; the children were so amazed by the flush toilet that they took it in turns to go to it throughout the night. I remember my mother laughing many a time when she told this story. As my father had always worked in the town as well as farming, he continued with his job and life settled down.

We started a new primary school and it was nothing like the old one. There were greater numbers of children for a start. I didn't really take to the headmaster or his way of working. While he went to the toilet, he would leave one of the primary seven children in charge, tasked with writing the name of anyone who spoke on the blackboard. He seemed to be gone for such a long time and then he came back smelling of strong cigarette smoke. He called any child with their name on the board up to the front and taking a ruler he gave them sharp slaps across their open hand. I still remember those children gasping and blinking and crying quietly when they went back to their desks. I had found myself in that position once, so I knew how they felt.

Although I had studied for it, I didn't pass my eleven plus exam — only one person in the class did.

Australia & America

Around this time, my father found out about the Assisted Passage Scheme to Australia. Australia was the land of milk and honey and we could go there for a small fee.

We were all set to go. A minister and his wife were to sponsor us until my father found a job. As well as working in a shop that sold furniture my father was an experienced carpet-fitter and would have had no trouble finding work.

The whole family had to have a medical, and being children we couldn't understand why the doctor hit our knees with a little hammer. Such was the discussion afterwards, and my mother told us he was testing our reflexes; we were still none the wiser.

We talked about Australia a lot, but my mother was becoming quieter during those discussions. The day the luggage labels arrived she finally told my father she wasn't going. She didn't want to leave her mother, mother-in-law and all that was familiar to her. I don't know what his reaction was at the time, but to this day he would tell you he thinks he, "could have made a go of it there."

Feeling unsettled, I suppose, my father decided we would move to a small farm in the country, not far from the town. Meanwhile, I started "big school." I was never really happy there. I was put into the A stream and it reminded me that I had come close to passing my eleven plus exam.

My brothers and sisters went to the local primary school, which was about two hundred yards from our home. They seemed content there. My mother was happy because she was living about two miles from her mother.

My grandmother had also moved after a hard winter. Although she was living in a much bigger cottage closer to the sea there were days when she had a faraway look in her eyes and I thought she was missing her little cottage in the hills. One night she passed away peacefully in her sleep. People said it was a lovely way to go. The reality for me was that I felt I would never see my grandmother again. We were all heartbroken. It was the first time I saw my father cry. Although he loved his own mother who lived in the town, he and my mother's mother were very fond of each other, they shared the same sense of humour.

My mother had great difficulty dealing with her grief. It took the form of a nervous rash on her face which the doctors found hard to heal. Eventually the rash disappeared and a smile came back into her lovely blue eyes which had been tearful for so long. Whether my father thought she needed a change of scene, I don't know, but after about a year he sold the farm and once again we moved into the town.

He was always trying to provide a better life for us. I don't know how he managed to save money with seven children, but he did. Often he would get me to count it with him before he lodged it in the bank. I knew he was proud of his achievements. Life settled down again, at least for a while.

There was great excitement when my father's brother came home from America for a holiday. He had done well for himself; he was foreman over a squad of twenty men who worked in the building trade. He had a good bungalow with a swimming pool and two cars. As he talked, my father listened attentively and after the children went to bed, the talk continued. My uncle told my father that if he decided to emigrate, he would give him a job and that we could live with his family until we found a house.

My father and mother talked about his proposal when my uncle returned to America. Feeling guilty she had prevented our immigration to Australia, my mother agreed that my father should go to America first and when he had settled in a job, the family would join him.

My parents decided my brother and I should go with my father and that the other five children would stay at home with my mother. Soon after, we set off — full of anticipation for the new life we were about to embark upon.

My father had been to England, but my brother and I had never been more than twenty miles from home. I was thirteen at the time and my brother was ten.

The flight seemed to take forever and when we finally arrived, I was sick for days. It must have been jet lag. We were all exhausted and certainly not ready for the welcome banners decorated with shamrocks and the celebration cake my aunt had kindly laid on for our arrival.

My aunt and uncle's bungalow was large with a big basement, which could be used by our family for as long as we needed it. While my brother and I were entertained by our cousins, my uncle showed my father around the area. He also showed him the job he had in mind for him as a plumber's mate.

On our third night, when the house was quiet, my father called me to the room he shared with my brother. He told me that he had made a terrible mistake and that he missed home. I could see how upset he was, but I was only thirteen years old and I wasn't sure how to deal with this news. I said, "You will have to give it a chance, Da. Stay until you start work and see how you feel." He put on a brave face during the day, but I could hear him sobbing quietly at night. The big strong man I had always looked up to was like a little child. He wanted my mother. He wanted home.

The next day, my brother and I sat quietly while he told my aunt and uncle he was sorry — this new life wasn't for him. They tried to tell him it was jet lag and he would be okay if he gave it a chance. They couldn't convince him and when they saw how upset he was, it was decided he needed to see the doctor. My poor dad had stopped eating and he was white as a sheet, he had no interest in talking about the future in America all he wanted to do was go home. It was obvious even to me that he was depressed. My aunt spoke to the doctor, and he said it would end up costing my father a fortune in medical bills if he stayed. It was homesickness and he needed to go home.

My father was so relieved he was going home, but it was time for a talk with me again. He told me he could afford flights home for my brother and himself but would I mind staying. He would go back home and work hard and send for me when he had saved the money for my flight. I was happy to stay. I would have been ashamed going back to school as the girls in my class would have known we had failed in our efforts to make a better life for ourselves. I think my father sensed my reluctance to return home so quickly.

I was happy for my father and my brother when we left them at the airport in Chicago, I knew it was for the best but I was quiet in the car on the way home with my aunt and uncle.

It suddenly dawned on me that I was far from my home and the family I had grown up with. I was in awe of the new country I had been left in. My aunt and uncle lived in the suburbs of the city but on our way home that day we travelled the freeway and it was bordered by huge fields that seemed to go on forever. I enquired what the tall crop was and I was told it was corn, it looked nothing like our corn at home and when I said this I was told it was sweetcorn.

These fields were so unlike the ones at home with their hedgerows of hawthorn and the violets and primroses growing underneath them and all the little birds and creatures making their homes there.

All along the freeway there were billboards advertising places to eat and things I had never heard of. The countryside was littered with fast food restaurants and Takeaways like Kentucky Fried Chicken and Roy Rodgers Roast Beef Sandwiches. I had never seen any of these at home. Open-air cinemas where cars drove into a parking lot for people to watch the movies and large stadiums where people gathered to watch the ballgames, these were forms of entertainment I hadn't been used to.

Attending school was quite an experience. Our day began by standing, hand on heart pledging allegiance to the flag of the United States of America. I had to learn and be able to answer questions on the Constitution of the USA. There was a strong focus on Sport, Music and Science Projects. I had a part in the school play; West Side Story.

The school was more modern in its decor than my school in Northern Ireland. There were water faucets in most of the corridors so students could get a drink between classes. The handsome American boys had lovely manners and they held the doors open for the girls. Yes, in other words it was a bit like Happy Days on television. My aunt pushed her children to learn and they had after hours activities like band practice, I was not expected to join in any of these. After all I would only be there until my father earned the money for my flight home.

My uncle was very good to me and he only lost his temper with me once. I didn't see the snake on the lawn when I was mowing the grass and I ran over it with the lawnmower. I don't think he was bothered about the dead snake or my screams, he was annoyed about the damage I had done to the lawnmower.

My aunt and I had a few arguments however. I will never forget the day I told her that Cassius Clay

(Muhammad Ali) should not have been sent to prison because he didn't want to go to war. She was really angry, I think her answer was "Your uncle did not come from this God-dam country and yet he fought in Vietnam."

In a gentler mood she told me how she met my uncle and I thought it was so romantic. They met on a train, he was in his army uniform and she was returning to the convent to take her final vows to become a nun. She fell in love with him and I could understand why, like my father he was a good looking man. She was a beautiful woman so it was no surprise that he fell in love with her. She had a smile like the sun but she also had a way of excluding you if she was annoyed with you about something.

In the beginning they didn't seem to be able to have children and they adopted a little girl. After that they had a girl and two boys of their own. I got on well with the children who were a few years younger than me. I grew quite fond of them but I knew that soon I would have to leave them. I had regular letters from home and the family told me they were missing me.

My father had been as good as his word, and although it must have been out of his comfort zone, he took a job in a factory. He worked all the hours he could, taking all the overtime he could get. Six months after he had gone home he sent the money for my airfare. I tearfully said goodbye to my American family at the airport. They had been very good to me but I felt that they had very little choice about taking me into their home and family

After a long flight from Chicago I missed the connecting flight from Shannon to Belfast. At thirteen I should never have been allowed to fly unaccompanied without supervision from the airport staff for the transfer. I had to spend the night in the Airport Hotel with strict instructions not to leave the room.

Alone in the hotel room for twelve hours, I had plenty of time to think. In the six months away from home I had grown up fast. I no longer felt like the child I had been when I left home. I had gone to school and my aunt and uncle had taken us on holidays while I had been staying with them. I had learned so much. Although I was excited about seeing my mother, father, brothers and sisters I couldn't help wondering how life would be once I was home again. I knew I had changed and life would never be the same as it was before I left.

Back Home In Northern Ireland

It was hard moving into a three-bedroom house in the Larne area again after the life I had been used to. My family was happy to see me and I was delighted to see them and give them the little gifts I had brought with me. I am ashamed to say that after a few days I wished I could go back to America. I had the good sense not to say so; my father had worked so hard to bring me back. I loved my family but there were nine of us and space was limited in the house.

I had been in America from March until September and the weather had been fantastic with sunshine and blue skies all summer. We had Barbecue Evenings and Pool Parties where we stayed out until it was dark, looking at the smouldering embers of the bonfire and the garden was lit by fire flies. I had returned to grey days and the lack of colour around me, evenings were spent in front of the television and it was as if my world had shrunk. I had had a taste of how the other half lived and I knew that someday I would travel, there was a whole world to see and I was living in a very small part of it. I couldn't wait until I was eighteen and I would be able to make my own choices.

I was a bit of a sensation at my old school, what with the American accent acquired after only six months. I had travelled and the girls in my class wanted to hear all about America. Needless to say, the novelty soon wore off and I continued the secretarial course I had started at school before I went away. For a couple of years I felt my life was quite boring. I was at that awkward age when I was neither an adult nor a child. I wasn't allowed a lot of freedom. My days were taken up with school, homework, household chores and helping my younger siblings with their homework. Once a week I would spend an hour at my friend's house or she would visit me. Occasionally we would go to the Regal Cinema to see a film.

Soon it was time to decide if I would go on to further education. Time for another wee talk with my father. He said, "I am leaving it up to you. You can get a better education, but there won't be a job good enough here in the town for you if you decide to do that. Your travel to Belfast for work will cost you a lot and it won't be worth your while working OR you can stay at home and look after the children and let your mother go out to work — she could earn more than you. We could get a better house and it would be a better life for all of us." Now I ask you, what would you have done? Of course, I took the option of looking after the children while my mother worked. I knew that my father only wanted the best for all of us. He had the rest of the family to consider, not just me. He had to look at the bigger picture and bringing up seven children wasn't easy. I also knew his heart was in the right place, he meant well but I did feel a bit envious of my friends who were going to the Technical College to complete their secretarial course.

My father had also said he would pay for me to take a typing course one night a week at night school. I accepted his offer, but the night of the exam I didn't go because I knew that my typing speed wasn't good enough; I had been using a typewriter only one night a week. However, after a year I applied for a job in the local department store. I started work on the cosmetics counter and when they heard I could type, I got the job as cashier and secretary. Perhaps the typing course had paid off after all. I had always known there was a God and I felt someone up there was looking after me.

I loved my work and I made friends easily, but life at home wasn't so easy. I wanted more freedom and being the eldest of seven I think my parents were setting a precedent as to how it would be for all of us. It was a case of, "this is my house and while you live here you will do as I say." At one point I left home for a while, I was sixteen, earning my own money and I didn't have to put up with being told what to do and the early curfew any longer. I shared a flat with two other girls, my mother was heartbroken and the reason I returned home eventually. I'm sure there were times when my father wished he had left me in America.

During my time away from home I started going to the Mormon Church or The Church of Latter Day Saints as it was known. I didn't realise it then but looking back I had become a seeker on the Spiritual Path. I was sixteen and I wanted to form my own opinions.

My parents were very angry but what they didn't realise was that the no drinking, no smoking and no sex before marriage policy of the religion kept me safe during that period of my life.

I was a reasonably good-looking girl and like my mother, I had won a couple of beauty competitions. In those days weekly dances were held in the local hotel and it was announced in advance that a beauty queen would be chosen. This was not something a girl applied for, judges selected a few girls from the dancers and short-listed them for an interview, choosing first, second and third. No one was more surprised than I was to find I had been chosen as Celebration Queen for the local football club one year and Festival Queen for the town the next. My parents were quite proud of that, but they weren't so keen on the fact that my looks attracted boyfriends. It was the early 1970s and there was a wonderful "going out" culture in the town. My friends and I worked hard all week and looked forward to going to dances two nights at the weekend. We didn't have a lot of money to spend but as long as we had a pair of jeans, a nice tee shirt and a lipstick and a comb in our back pocket all we needed was the entrance fee and the money for a Coca Cola. The Laharna Hotel brought fantastic Country and Western groups like *The Indians* and *Brian Coll and the Buckaroos* to the town.

We went there for the dancing and the girls were happy to dance together in groups. It was a brave boy who would interrupt and ask one of us to dance with him. For this reason the boys usually waited to the end of a set of three dances when we were having a break and they approached our group in pairs. One boy chose the girl he fancied and his friend settled for a dance with one of the others. Saturday night was disco night in the Kings Arms Hotel. Disco was a new craze sweeping the province and we thought we were so cool going there. We dressed up more and we altered our style of dancing to fit in with the crowd. We didn't jive, we copied the dancers on Top of the Pops on television.

Before I had left home I met my first boyfriend,

he was from farming stock, and I thought that would have been a point in his favour. Something didn't please my father about this boy, though — he was slightly built and a few inches shorter than me. "You need to start with the frame of a man," my father said.

After that, the hints about his height came often. My boyfriend and I had watched a Dracula film with the family one night and after he left, my father said, "Would that be a boy who could save you from Dracula?" I didn't answer but I realised my father might have a point, my boyfriend would not have been a match for Dracula! Next he told me he saw my boyfriend in the bank and he was standing on his tiptoes to see over the counter. Yes, he had worn me down and I finished the relationship.

Next came the son of a millionaire, but he didn't fare any better in the popularity stakes. His time-keeping wasn't good, according to my father. "If a man arrives fifteen minutes late to take you out, he is showing a lack of respect for you," he told me. There were also one or two casual ones who left me home from dances, but I didn't bring them into the house.

Then along came THE ONE. His name was Daniel, I was sixteen and he was almost twenty-one. He was tall, dark and handsome with a beard and the bluest eyes I had ever seen — there was kindness and gentleness in those eyes. He also dressed well and had good manners. In fact, he was just the sort of boy a girl could take home to meet her parents. When I met him he was just about to go to sea as an engineer, and even though I knew he was going to be away for about five months at a time, I fell in love with him.

I took him home to meet my family and he got on well with them. I met his family and they were lovely, he had three brothers and two sisters, all younger than him. His parents were kind to me and I could see he came from a loving home. He went to sea and I missed him terribly and later, when he asked me to marry him I didn't hesitate.

We got married the day after my eighteenth birthday. By then my father had a house near the coast with an uninterrupted view of the sea, something he had been working for all his life. He had achieved his dream for the family. Daniel and I were married in the Presbyterian Church he attended and we had our wedding reception in Ballygally Castle. It was a lovely day with our family and friends.

We had a short honeymoon in the Isle of Man. It was a popular destination in those days because of the close proximity to Northern Ireland and the regular ferries to the Island. Young men loved it because it was well known for the famous TT Races. That is how we spent our honeymoon, travelling at speed around the Motorcycle course in a hired car. Daniel was in his element! I loved him so much I was happy to see him happy.

I had packed a suitcase for one week and when I returned my sisters had shared the rest of my clothes between them! They thought I didn't want them or I would have taken them with me. My poor husband had married me and I was almost destitute.

We moved in with his great aunt for a few weeks, she lived in a house in Chichester Avenue in Belfast. It was kind of her to take us in but the house was quiet and if I am honest I found it a bit spooky. We missed our families and ended up visiting them rather a lot.

All At Sea

Soon I was packing my suitcase again. Daniel was joining an oil tanker in Tilbury, England and sailing to the Persian Gulf and as his wife I was allowed to travel with him.

We had a lovely cabin on board and while he was on watch I spent my time sunbathing and talking to the other wives. There was a good ship's library and I had also taken embroidery and knitting with me to pass the time.

Meal times were in the saloon and dinner consisted of seven courses with silver service. The ship had an Indian crew and the stewards were immaculately dressed in white uniforms. I had very little work to do, keeping our cabin clean and doing our laundry didn't take a lot of effort. Although I made a point of walking a few circuits of the deck each day, I still managed to put on about a stone in weight during that time.

Our entertainment consisted mainly of watching old fashioned reels of films and playing board games. We had party nights and like the other wives I took my turn behind the bar serving drinks. We danced to the music of Neil Diamond, Carol King, The Carpenters, The Seekers and Dr. Hook.

During the day I loved to go up to the bow of the ship and watch the flying fish, I was fascinated the first time I saw them. We saw sperm whales one morning at sunrise and like a few other sights I have seen, they are stored like photographs in my memory. Something spoke to my soul as I sat there on the bow surrounded by ropes looking out to sea, whether it was because of the vastness of it and the rhythmic waves I don't know. There was peace and it reminded me of the phrase, "the peace that surpasses all understanding." In that moment I knew that someone had created all of this, that someone had also created me to be a part of it and appreciate it.

There was a certain loneliness on the voyage, the men talked of their work on board ship and places they had worked ashore, and those were conversations I couldn't really get involved in. I was only eighteen and at that point I was not a world traveller like most of them. It was easier for me to smile, remain quiet and listen.

Our captain was from Larne and he was great fun. I can still hear his hearty laughter booming out when I think of him. Just in case the four wives should get bored he came up with a plan for us to do our steering tickets. This meant we would take control of the ship's wheel and steer to a given course. We had to spend ten hours in total at the wheel, spread out over a few evenings. He joined us on the bridge for this and his jokes had us laughing most of the time. If we turned the wheel quickly he would say we had spilled everyone's drinks in the bar. He came up one time and asked me how my head was. I said, "It's not so bad now, it was sore earlier on." He roared with laughter, it was a term for asking how my direction was. The wives did not disgrace themselves, we received our Board of Trade certificates to say we were capable of steering tankers of a certain tonnage.

We left the ship on a launch at Ras al Khaimah for our transfer to Dubai and I really didn't know what to expect. The men wore long white robes and white or checked headgear. I became aware of some of them staring at me and I felt uncomfortable, I decided I would not meet their gaze and instead stared fixedly at the floor. I loved seeing the children, the boys in their long gowns and skull caps speaking this foreign language I was not used to.

We stayed overnight in a hotel and I had never seen anywhere as opulent, it had white marble floors and pillars topped with gold, a lot of the furniture was embellished with gold also and everywhere there were plants reminiscent of the jungle. It looked like a palace with its long low velvet sofas and ottomans. I remember wondering what the meat was when we were having dinner and Daniel said, "It might be camel." I didn't know whether he was joking but I lost my appetite for it. Strange how we are happy to eat one animal but not another.

When we flew home we couldn't get to sleep the first night, it was too quiet. We had been used to the constant hum of the ships' engine and the air conditioning as well as the general noise of living with so many others. Laughing, Daniel said, "I wish someone would bang on a drum or something." We soon got used to the peace again and slept like logs.

**

I had a second trip with Daniel, this time joining the ship in Kharg Island in the Persian Gulf and sailing to the U.K. His trips usually lasted for four and a half months and then he had two months leave. We had no idea what life held in store for us. Very soon the unthinkable would happen.

Life on board started in much the same way as before, this time with a larger ship and a mixed crew. It was a strange life with no children or senior citizens on board. Soon I found myself talking to Daniel about wanting to settle and have a child. I remember telling him a bambino would make our lives perfect, I hadn't really stopped to think that I would be at home alone with a baby while he went to sea. An oil tanker was no place for a child and children were not allowed on board.

We were considering all of this and I had just finished making a new dress for a party night on board when the captain sent for Daniel. A telegram had arrived to say his youngest sister who was eight years old had died as result of an accident. Words cannot explain how we felt. Even now I can't bring myself to think about it. Daniel had to continue the trip as a replacement for him could not be found before the ship sailed again.

I left the ship in Germany and flew home to be met at the airport by his poor father. His mother cried in my arms the following day. I found myself ill prepared to cope with their grief, I was nineteen and I had no experience apart from my beloved grandmother's death. I wanted to say all the right things but I didn't know what to say. How do you comfort someone who has just lost their child? I was upset for Daniel, who was unable to get home to his family after hearing the news.

I spent the next few weeks until his return with my mother who had just came out of hospital after a serious operation. Each day we took short walks together, going a little further each time as part of her convalescence. My mother recovered quickly, she had to, as she had a family to look after and work to return to.

I felt it was a time I would never want to go through again but my feelings were nothing compared to those of Daniel and his family. His father died within a year from a heart attack but many of us felt he died of a broken heart.

My mother-in-law lost her daughter, husband and mother within three years, I don't know how she coped. Although Daniel and his brother were both married she had three more children of school age so somehow she managed to go on with life. Not only did she have the children to look after, she brought her elderly aunt to live with her. She looked after her for the next twenty seven years. My mother-in-law was the most unselfish person I have ever met.

At the beginning of our marriage we rented a cottage from Daniel's grandmother. On his return from sea after his sister passed away we decided to buy our own home. We found out there was a development of new bungalows being built in Ballyclare, a town about ten miles from our families and we paid the deposit for our house. When we took possession of it, Daniel had two months leave and in that time we made our new home as comfortable as we could.

We had been through so much together. I was

only twenty and so much had happened. Daniel returned to sea for a while but managed to be at home later for the birth of our first son. Our beautiful baby boy, who would be company for me for a long time to come, changed my life. Now I had a little soul depending on me. There were times when I wished Daniel was home with us, and although some of my siblings stayed with me occasionally, I was lonely.

We had been living in our first house for a short time when Daniel's grandmother passed away. His family home was quite close to hers and we decided we would buy her house and renovate it. Just before we moved, I discovered I was pregnant and we moved into a little caravan on the property with our two year-old son while the work was being done.

We worked hard to make sure the house was ready to move into as quickly as possible, and our second son was born just before his dad went back to sea. He resembled my side of the family and it reminded me of holding my brothers and sisters as babies.

When our new little son was just a couple of months old there was a shock in store for me, my father and mother separated! They were coming up to their 25th wedding anniversary and it was totally unexpected. It felt like the end of the world and that they would never be happy again. However, in the future, after their divorce they went on to meet and marry new partners and of course they were happy again.

Since this was their story I don't feel free to tell it. It is hard to remain impartial when it is your parents, at the time, the family were devastated. I had two small children and a husband at sea. I found it hard to cope with. I had the most wonderful mother-in-law anyone could have wished for, and she was very supportive. It also helped that the new baby was such a good little boy.

After about a year my father met a lovely woman and they got married soon after. Child rearing took over my life. The boys started playschool at three years old and primary school at four. They also joined the cub scouts and I found myself busy most of the time.

My mother had moved to the Isle of Man and it was the perfect place for the boys and me to spend our summer holidays. It was lovely to see her and it gave her a chance to see the children. I remember one time she met us as we came off the Isle of Man boat and she was wearing a beautiful blue jersey dress, her hair was done to perfection and yes, she was wearing her lipstick. I still thought I had the nicest looking mummy, just as I had twenty years earlier when she collected me from school. She met her new partner in the Isle of Man and after a few years they returned to live in Larne. I was glad because we were able to visit them all the time. It was good having her home.

While Daniel was away the children and I had lots of days out, travelling to Portrush on the north coast of Antrim or to Carrickfergus Castle where I later became a Tour Guide. We went to the beach and also visited family and friends or we went shopping. The times spent with my mother were the best because I no longer felt solely responsible for the care of the children.

The first time I went to the Isle of Man I hired a car and after that I took my own car. Driving around there reminded me of being on honeymoon and I missed Daniel even more.

I made friends with some of the other mums who lived in my area. One day I had a phone call from a mum called Jan who sounded upset, she said, "Your son lent my wee boy a pencil with a little frog on top and the frog has jumped into the fire, where did you get it so I can replace it?" I laughed so much that she joined in and although I didn't know it then that was the beginning of a friendship which continues some forty years later. She and her husband have been the kind of friends you don't see for ages yet when you meet up it is as if you have never been apart.

Although I was the one they spent most of their time with, the boys loved their dad coming home and life changed for a couple of months every time he returned. Then, just as we were used to him being there, he would go away again. Although I wanted to ask Daniel to leave the sea, I never did because I didn't want him to blame me for spoiling his life.

When the boys were about seven and five years old, Daniel's company offered Voluntary Selective Severance and he took it and came home to us. After a few months, he got a job with a local company. They asked him to go to work in Saudi Arabia and he jumped at the chance. Once again, I was alone with the children.

I persevered for a while, but one day I found myself wondering if we should split up and go our separate ways. What would my life look like? I realized I would still be in the kitchen cooking dinner for my boys. Besides, I loved Daniel and I decided I would stay in the marriage. At that point, I told him how unhappy I was, and he came home for good. He took a job locally and apart from the occasional short trip for work, we have never been apart since. Our relationship has grown stronger over the years.

Once again we moved house — perhaps I had the wanderlust of my father. A beautiful big house in our area came up for sale. At first sight, it was way out of our price range. It was also much too big for us. The agent told us, however, that it had been repossessed and we could just about afford it.

The new house had five bedrooms, three bathrooms, dining room, kitchen, utility room and a lounge that seemed the size of a football pitch compared to what we were used to. It also had a recreation room with built-in bar in the basement and views to die for from every level. We took my father with us to view it, as we wanted his opinion and we knew it would please him if he was invited. He thought it would be a big undertaking and said it would cost at least ten thousand pounds to carpet it. Later that evening he phoned to see if we had made a decision; he couldn't believe it when I said we were pricing carpets for it! I think he was proud of us in his own way, for taking it on.

Once we moved in, we realized it would take a lot of work to bring it up to the standard we required. We were young and neither of us was afraid of hard work, so we spent the first six months sanding and repainting the walls. Daniel used a chisel to scrape the old dark varnish off the wooden window frames. The frames had small panes, so it was a mammoth task.

As we sorted out the problems in the house, I began to appreciate Daniel being an engineer — and a good one too. He saved us a lot of money by doing everything himself. I worked hard as well. I was the "ideas woman" having always loved interior design and I enjoyed it when friends complimented us on the difference we were making to the place.

After the first winter we also discovered that a big house has bigger bills — it cost a lot to heat it! However, it was one of the happiest times in our lives and we had some wonderful parties in the bar with family and friends.

Our boys were growing up fast and we were proud of how well they were getting on with their education. They were good boys and didn't give us too much trouble. Finding out they were smoking didn't go down well with us, but apart from that, all was going well.

When we had been in the house for a while I wanted nice things for it, so I told Daniel I was going to get myself a job. I began working as a tour guide in Carrickfergus Castle and the money was good. The job was a temporary contract for three months but I talked so much they kept me for two years. It was an amazing job, imagine talking all day and getting paid for it! After learning the history of the castle I was well prepared for taking the various groups around. When I took the preschool children around I was like a child along with them. Almost every school in the province visited as they were either being taught about Homes through the Ages or The Normans at that time.

Anyone who visited Northern Ireland seemed to come to the castle and I was fortunate enough to meet people from all over the world. There were weddings in the little chapel, children's parties in the dungeons, exhibitions and banquets in the Keep. The people I worked with were born raconteurs and there was never a dull moment.

Things were going well at home as our boys were in their teens and capable of being left alone. I finished work at four in winter and six in summer so the hours suited me. There were a few times when I was tired as it was a five and a half day week but we managed to keep things running smoothly at home. I loved that job and I cried when I had to leave, but my contract had come to an end and nothing could be done. I had been so used to working with the public. What would I do now?

We had a couple of extra bedrooms in the house and stunning views, so we knew it would be ideal for tourists seeking accommodation. I took a small business course and with the help of the Tourist Board, I offered country house accommodation. I had no idea how hard the work would be!

At first, it was really exciting! I went on a spending spree for new towels and bed linens, then we decorated the two bedrooms and bathroom on the top floor of the house. We had enough furniture and the rooms had built-in wardrobes. New televisions and tea trays completed the guest rooms. We had a lovely dining room that we didn't use a lot; it was beside the kitchen and perfect for breakfast for the guests.

The first year, we had few visitors, but business soon picked up. It was the year of the Peace Process in Northern Ireland, which opened up the flood gates for tourists from all over the world. There were so many tourists that we had to help find them accommodation with others who were offering Bed and Breakfast. Business soon levelled out and, although I worked hard, we could never have survived on the money coming in if Daniel had not been the main breadwinner.

It was a lot of fun over the years and each year we couldn't wait to see who would arrive. We were lucky. We always seemed to have lovely people staying with us. We also had repeat business and we got to know people well.

I employed a girl to help me with the cleaning one time, but she took the summer off to be with her children when they were on holiday from school. Summer was my busiest time, so I decided to work alone after that. In the winter months we sometimes hosted contractors who were working in the area. I had to cook an evening meal for them and often found myself working until ten o'clock. I had to be up at six in the morning, seven days a week. When things quietened down, we were able to plan a well-deserved holiday, which I looked forward to very much. Until that time, we had mostly gone on family holidays — camping with the boys around the UK and Ireland or venturing abroad to Menorca, Tenerife and Rhodes with them.

It was time to leave the boys behind. Besides, they had no desire to leave their girlfriends.

The Gambia

When we booked a holiday to the Gambia, I had no idea what lay ahead. My friend, Elizabeth, once observed that all holiday destinations were so alike. "I swear if someone set you down somewhere with your eyes closed, and you opened them you couldn't tell the difference between one place and another," she said. She was about to find out that could not be said of the Gambia.

We were a party of four — Daniel and I with our two best friends, John and Elizabeth. Daniel had known John and Elizabeth for most of his life and I had known them for over twenty years. This was our second couple's holiday abroad together. We had spent a happy time in Tenerife the year before, and we knew our friendship could stand the test of being together for a couple of weeks. Goodness knows why we didn't take a package holiday to Spain like everyone else! I suppose it was time for an adventure.

We travelled from Belfast to Manchester, where we spent the night in a Guest House recommended by friends. The lady of the house could not have been more welcoming; not only did she store our winter clothes for our return, but she took us to the airport for our flight to The Gambia. We arrived in West Africa in the late afternoon, full of anticipation for what lay ahead.

We were on board the minibus on our way to the hotel when I experienced what could only be described as a culture shock. We were passing through a village of little huts. Some of them appeared to have only three walls and a roof and from what I could see, there was nothing but poverty all around. Some of the little shacks seemed to be serving food. John said, "Maybe we should come out here for a meal some night." I thought he was crazy, and longed for the bus to reach the hotel.

It was then I saw them; three young black men, their dark skins glistening in the sun, working together. They were putting three wheels on an old Transit van and it didn't even have an engine. I began to cry at the futility of it. I remember thinking had I known I would feel like this I would not have come on this holiday. I looked at Daniel and he appeared to be coping better than I was. He had seen similar scenes on his work travels. Elizabeth and John were smiling, taking in everything that was happening. Was I the only one feeling like this?

I knew very little about Africa but I felt our holiday would be more like the ones people had in the beautiful safari lodges I had seen on television. Soon we reached the hotel, which was like something from an old movie. The buildings were shaped like temples at the front and painted a dull shade of pink. Once we passed through the main buildings, the bedrooms were to be found in long, two storey blocks. The gardens were beautiful with palm trees and tropical plants around a swimming pool. The beach ran parallel to the gardens with a fence in between. I noted the security guard in uniform and felt a little uneasy, but I comforted myself with the knowledge he was there for our safety.

I followed Daniel up the flight of steps to our room. It was sparsely furnished with a bed surrounded by mosquito netting, a chest of drawers and a fifties style wardrobe painted with African symbols. A couple of chairs completed the furnishings. We also had our own bathroom. Luxury did not describe the living accommodation, but I decided to make the best of it. We unpacked and dressed for dinner.

Soon the clothes were sticking to our bodies and we accepted the fan we were offered to rent. We also decided we would have a fridge to share with our friends.

The dining room was like something from a Somerset Maugham novel — a long, low building with tongue and groove boarded walls painted in eau de nil green. Large ceiling fans constantly whirred and the sound of African drums reverberated around the room. There was a wall of windows and my attention was drawn time and time again to the view of water with white wading birds. The whole scene felt surreal.

After dinner on the first night, we had a couple of drinks and walked towards our rooms — we had to be careful not to step on the frogs on the steps. Laughing, Daniel and I closed the door to our room quickly in case the frogs would get inside. Finally in bed under the mosquito netting, I surveyed the room and felt I had never stayed in a stranger place.

Next morning everything looked brighter. Opening the window shutters, the view revealed a little market about two hundred yards away. It was full of stalls and from that distance I could see fabrics in jewel colours. A young man moved towards the back of the market which meant he was facing in my direction. What I saw next made me jump away from the window, but not before he had spotted me. It was obvious that the wall behind the market was an outdoor toilet for the men! At that point, I gave up all hope of sitting out on the little balcony.

We dressed and joined the others for breakfast, comparing the mosquito bites we had been afflicted with despite the mosquito netting around the bed. Within a couple of days Elizabeth's bites were raised in huge water blisters. Mine didn't look so bad, but they itched and irritated like crazy.

After breakfast we decided we would go to the capital, Banjul. It was, even by Northern Irish standards, a small town and I felt uncomfortable because I had not had the foresight to wear a long skirt. I was dressed in shorts and what with my lily white legs, it was no wonder that people were staring.

A taxi driver offered us his services and we gladly accepted. He stayed with us the whole time and proudly acted as our guide. He was friendly and talked about his family. I remember very little about the town but I do remember going into a little shop that sold part bottles of shampoo, shower gel and other bits and pieces the tourists had left behind. We paid the driver, gave him a good tip and a bag of sweets for his children. We were rewarded with a beautiful smile and a promise to be available to take us out anywhere we wanted to go.

After a light lunch, we went to the beach. A couple of people were offering freshly squeezed orange juice and of course I accepted gratefully. Women with colourful long dresses and turbans carried trays of fruit on their heads and boys selling postcards approached the tourists in the hope they would buy some. We were told that there was a better beach to be found if we crossed a sandy area when the tide was out. Daniel and I ventured across the sand one afternoon and we had to run between hundreds of tiny crabs. Eventually we came to the beautiful deserted beach — we had it to ourselves for the rest of the afternoon.

Elizabeth and John wanted to see a bit more life going on around them and their taxi driver took them to another beach almost every day. They became friendly with a Scottish couple on one of these adventures. Arriving back at the hotel one day, they asked Daniel and me if we would like to go up to a safari camp in the jungle with the couple. Being the cautious type I said, "How do you know you can trust them?" Elizabeth assured me, they were both Christians and their two small children would be travelling along with them. This was her guarantee that we would be safe. She arranged for them to come to our hotel so we could meet them. They turned out to be a very nice couple and we got on well together, we made plans to go with them that weekend.

Meanwhile we had become friendly with the young gardener at the hotel. He changed the little tropical flower arrangement every day and loved to come and talk while we were in the gardens. He invited us to his house to meet his wife and his new baby, but regretfully we were unable to go because his day off work coincided with the trip we were about to take. He later told us he had called his son Lamin and that Daniel was his second name. For a long time to come we would tease my husband that there was a little Daniel running around in The Gambia We were excited about the weekend to come and if I am honest I was a little bit nervous. Perhaps seeing all those episodes of Tarzan as a child had had an effect!

Before heading to the jungle, we took a bus tour one evening to sample the local nightlife. We were taken to a couple of little bars. The guide described what I took to be a nightclub, but when we arrived, it was just a bar with people drinking and a couple of young men dancing to light patterns on the floor made by a laser pointer. The music was coming from a tape player and the dancers had great rhythm. Again I was reminded that the people had so little and yet they made the most of what they had. Earlier I had watched some men exercise on the beach and they were weight lifting with two paint cans filled with concrete and joined by an old iron bar. It is true what they say; necessity really is the mother of invention.

The day of our jungle trip found us all in good spirits, looking forward to the adventure. We joined the family of four and the owner of the safari camp, who was to be our driver. Ahead of us was a six-hour drive up river to the jungle area, where we were to stay for a couple of nights.

Sitting in the back of an open Land Rover with an inch thick of foam cushion under your bottom over dirt roads in the hot sun is not to be recommended. We had been told to bring only a change of clothes. We took two bottles of soft drinks and two bags of sweets and lollipops for the children. We took very little money assuring ourselves we could get some when we got to Georgetown.

Going slowly through some of the villages the Land Rover was followed by lots of beautiful children. They had skin the colour of ebony and short curly hair, their magnificent smiles showing lovely white teeth. They called "minty, minty." I didn't understand until our driver said, "They want sweets." Minutes later they were scrambling around after the handfuls of sweets we threw. The other thing they wanted was pens or pencils. Again the driver explained, he said if they had a pen or a pencil they could go to school. The children had so little, and yet they seemed happy. Elizabeth gave a little boy a small amount of Coca Cola in a bottle and he jumped in jubilation, tasted the coke, didn't like it and, after pouring it out, he ran delightedly to his mother to give her the bottle.

At the halfway point on our journey, we stopped at a little village to use the long drop toilets and have something to eat. By now I was not surprised to enter the little tin shed and find the toilet was a hole in the ground that one had to straddle over. On leaving the toilet a boy was standing with a little tin can of water, which he poured over my hands. I was grateful for this.

Elizabeth and Daniel lost their appetites when we were told to sample three pots of goat stew and say which one we wanted to have for lunch. They were adamant they couldn't stomach it and eagerly accepted egg rolls instead. A plastic bag containing bread rolls and two dead flies was produced and the dirtiest knife I have ever seen was used to cut them and sort of mash the eggs onto them. The rolls were folded in two and they were given one each. John and I felt we had fared better with the goat stew — at least it was hot and there was less chance of germs.

We knew we were to have another stop and, assuming it would be a large town, we attempted to tidy ourselves up. We also wanted to get money there, but we were disappointed to find only a general store. Soap was cut up and sold from a large block, whilst candles and rolls of fabric sat beside floor brushes. There was also a few groceries and fruit and vegetables. It was no large town, but we managed to get some money exchanged to pay the owner of the safari camp.

When we finally reached the camp, my hair was thick with dust and stiff as a board. My limbs were brown, but I wasn't sure if it was suntan or dirt. Elizabeth, wearing a pair of white shorts that were brown with dust said, "Morna, I have never seen you looking worse." Laughing, I said, "You're no oil painting yourself." Daniel and John, wearing beige clothes, suited their surroundings and looked better than when we started our journey.

When we reached the camp, I felt dehydrated and unwell. The others went for a swim in a green, murky swimming pool with dead bugs floating on top of the water; there was no way I was putting my body in there. We had been given little huts with thatched roofs for two people, and I couldn't wait to go inside. The beds were built from concrete with a thin foam mattress on top, but I would have been glad to lie anywhere. Someone decided I needed salt because of the heat but what I really needed was lots of water.

Evening came and we all went to the main hut for dinner. We had been told to be careful as there were three foot lizards and snakes in the area around the camp. I can't remember what we ate but I do remember when we got back to our hut there were frogs everywhere. The boys who worked there came in and put them out and sprayed the place with insecticide in case of mosquitos.

Daniel took a toilet roll and with scrunched up bits of paper filled every hole he could find. I asked why he was doing it and he said, "If a frog can get in just think what else can get in." Looking at the candle and matches by the bedside, I prayed I wouldn't need to use the small bathroom in the middle of the night. It was just as well I didn't because the next day Daniel discovered the plumbing was not connected outside and the frogs were coming up the toilet. I wasn't too happy about using the toilet after that.

We had been told the generator was to be turned off at midnight to conserve electricity. We settled down and, to begin with, it was hard getting to sleep. It was so dark and silent until suddenly there would be the sound of something scuffling about on the thatched roof —probably the massive tree rats. And every now and then, there was a terrible screech from an animal being caught. At one point something smacked me in the face; I think it was a large moth. Tiredness after the long journey soon overtook me and I slept like a log. Elizabeth said she had done the same. John and Daniel didn't sleep a wink. Perhaps they felt they were our protectors.

We had been told to rise early and go down to the boat on the river as it was the best place to watch the dawn. We sat on the seats of an unstable boat watching the mist rise from the river, listening to the jungle coming alive. It was the most amazing experience. The birdsong was the first to be heard, a little later when the chattering of the monkeys reached a crescendo, we knew it was time for breakfast. We had quite a satisfying breakfast of orange juice, cereal, miniature sugary doughnuts and coffee.

We spent the most wonderful day on the river. At one point we were told to be quiet because there were about five or six hippos close by. They were circling a baby hippo, which meant they felt threatened. Hippos, we learned, kill more people than crocodiles every year, so we were glad to leave the area to them.

As it became dark, we sprayed our bodies with Bop to protect us from the mosquitos and headed for a small, lit up jetty. Returning to our huts we discovered our clothes from the day before had been so well washed and ironed that the pattern had nearly disappeared from my tee shirt. We had dinner and drinks and everyone slept better the second night.

The next morning we were up early again and after breakfast we waited by the Land Rover for all of our party to assemble. As we waited some Gambian women who were doing their washing at the river came into view. They started pointing and laughing at Elizabeth, possibly because she looked unusual to them — fair-haired, small, slim and wearing shorts and a sun top. John, seeing the women in their lovely colourful clothes held up the video camera, but one woman became quite annoyed. She said, "Don't videoize me." Our driver explained that they think if you do this you can capture their soul.

We were staying in the area known as Janjanbureh, formerly known as McCarthy Island, which was once known for the slave trade. Our plans for the day were to visit the town formerly known as Georgetown. We went to a market, but the smells were hard to bear while we walked around in the heat. I turned at one point and came face to face with a cow's head. Fish, fruit and vegetables were also for sale, but there were so many flies I couldn't wait to leave. A little girl came up and stroked our skin; we were told it was because she had never seen a white person before and she wanted to see if a white person's skin felt the same as hers.

We moved to a quieter part of the town and there, in front of us, was a Methodist Church. One of the local boys climbed through a window and opened the door for us. The minister arrived and gave him an awful telling off for being disrespectful and breaking into his church. Inside, the church was very old and painted white with a few rows of dark wooden pews. It was quite basic with a pulpit at the front. Bats were obviously protected because there was a pile of bat poo and the stench was overpowering. No attempt seemed to have been made to fill the hole that was high up on the wall where they were entering. How people were able to sit through a church service, I couldn't imagine.

As we walked around, lots of local children joined us. I was wearing a long green floral skirt, a short sleeved top and a white hat to keep the sun off my head. Elizabeth said that surrounded by the children, I looked like a missionary. She found this very funny.

Next we were taken to the slave pens and the market place where slaves had been sold. It is thought that approximately 5000 slaves a year were shipped from the Gambia in the 17th and 18th centuries. There were manacles and chains on the walls. While we were there we were told the story of the Freedom Tree. A little distance from the market stood a tree and if a slave managed to run to it and touch it, they had their freedom. My heart lifted with hope until I heard that underneath the tree sat a man with a rifle to make sure they didn't make it. The slaves' only chance came when he was asleep. I found the very thoughts of those times sickening. I was glad that slavery had been abolished in 1833 but it was a pity it had continued for so long.

Soon our trip was over, and it was time to leave the Safari Camp. I was looking forward to returning to Banjul and what I now deemed to be the comfort

of our hotel. On the long journey back we were un-
usually quiet.

I thought of our trip, everything we had seen and
done, and I knew it was a trip like no other. People
there had so little, living mostly in villages in family
groups. In the evenings, a fire was lit at the edge of
the village and the cooking pot was put on. People
contributed whatever they had and they shared dinner. For all of that long journey through the Gambia
I hadn't seen a child without a smile, yet they had so
little compared with the children at home, it must
have been a case of what you never had you never
miss. This reminded me of my early childhood and
the fact that we didn't go away on holidays, what you
never had you never miss. I had no idea when I was
taking pennies into school for the poor children in
Africa that I would one day go there.

**

Life at the hotel returned to normal with sunbathing
by the pool or on the beach, meeting up with
Elizabeth and John for dinner and drinks to discuss
the day's events and have a few laughs. One night we
decided to have room service for dinner together in
our room. We had a lovely meal, each having chosen
what we wanted. After dinner John and Elizabeth
went to their own room and it was then that John
took really ill and the doctor had to be called.

Nobody really knew what it was but we put it down to food poisoning from the prawns he had for dinner.

When I travel it usually takes me about three days to acclimatise and I had been looking forward to the second week of the holiday when I would be used to the heat and the itching of the mosquito bites. Week two started off as a lovely, happy time with lots of talk about our adventure in the jungle. We met the couple who had taken us up there and they took us to their rented house and also showed us the house they were building. They took us to see the Crocodile Pool, and although we were assured it was a sacred pool and the crocodiles were perfectly safe I was not about to walk among them although John seemed happy to do so. I still don't know the secret of why they just lay there and didn't attack. Were they well fed before we came? Had someone put a spell on them?

We spent a couple of days relaxing and enjoying lying in the sun after all the excitement we had experienced. One day we took a walk to the little market near the hotel. I stopped at one of the stalls and a young woman studying my top asked, "Can I have your bra?" I said to the others, "Why would she want my bra —it wouldn't fit her?" My bra was a size 38G. One of my travelling companions suggested, "Maybe she wants to carry her shopping home in it!"

Not being one to take offence easily, I joined the laughter. The stall holder said, "I want it for my sister. She has no bra." I felt sad and made a mental note to give it to her before we went home. The people would be able to use everything we could do without.

The following day I was struck down with a stomach bug. I was so ill with pains in my tummy and even though I was drinking plenty of water to make sure I didn't become dehydrated, I got worse instead of better. I struggled to get out of bed. I was drawing into myself and I didn't want the others, including Daniel, around. I just wanted to be left alone. Elizabeth and John came to meet up with us to go for dinner and I said, "I can't go but I am begging the three of you to go. I will be ok."

After they left I became disoriented and could hear a mayday call from a plane. I knew if I didn't get closer to the fan in the room, I was in trouble. Using all the energy I had left, I threw myself across the bed nearer to the fan. I started to shiver as the cold air hit me, but I persevered and, by the time the others returned, I knew I was on the road to recovery. Later my GP at home told me it was a reaction to the Lariam tablets I was taking to prevent Malaria. Not knowing that at the time, I had continued taking the tablets regardless; I'd had mosquito bites and the risk of malaria could have been great.

Returning from her meal that night Elizabeth said, "Thank God you are okay. I cried when I left you earlier. Your face was the same colour as the mosquito netting surrounding the bed. You looked as if you had been laid out after death and I thought you would die here and not return home with us." It seemed that I had a lucky escape and for that I was truly grateful. I wasn't ready for heaven just yet. I had a lot more living to do. Besides, I had two lovely sons waiting for me at home.

**

Soon it was time to return home. The holiday was over. We sat at the airport and argued over whose turn it was to use the little battery operated personal fan I had brought with me. This was the fan they had laughed at when it was checked at the airport on the way from Belfast. We talked about our holiday in the Gambia. Did any of us regret our time there? Quite a lot had happened to us since we arrived and not all of it was good. The answer was a resounding no; we didn't regret going.

This had been a holiday like no other, one we would never forget. We would dine out on it for years to come and here I am twenty years later writing about it as if it was yesterday. I know that The Gambia is nothing like it was then; progress has crept in and changed it. Browsing travel brochures,

I can see that the hotel looks grand and the Safari Camp has closed.

We went on to have other holidays with John and Elizabeth, but none was as adventurous as the trip to the Gambia. I decided that after this West African holiday, I would never miss another opportunity to go on my travels.

Colourful Cuba

The following year we continued working just as hard as previously. We had a wide variety of nationalities staying with us and we did our best to make it a home away from home for them.

At one point five Italians who were working in the area came to stay with us. They didn't speak English and I had to attempt speaking Italian with the help of a phrase book. It wasn't easy but we laughed our way through it.

During their stay I took one week off and went to Corfu for a holiday with a friend, leaving my poor husband in charge. He was able to prepare continental breakfast for them but I had arranged for them to have dinner elsewhere. I came back feeling refreshed, the holiday had been just what I needed. They had been with us for quite a few months and the only break I got from cooking was when we took them to an Italian Restaurant in Carrickfergus. Another night our wonderful friends, Hazel and Ivor invited them to come with us to their house for a meal. I don't think they will ever know how much I appreciated it at the time. Hazel is a fantastic cook and the evening was a great success. Soon after that it was time for the Italians to go home and although it had been nice having them stay it was a great relief when I didn't have to speak in broken English and even more broken Italian.

Winter was fast approaching and we hadn't booked our holiday. While we were having drinks with John and Elizabeth one night I jokingly asked Daniel, "Where are you taking us on holiday this year?" After The Gambia we knew that we were ready for another adventure. Cuba was one of the winter sun destinations and it sounded a bit more exciting than a lot of the other places we looked at in the holiday brochures. We knew about Cuba's history as a communist country and we had heard of Fidel Castro and the famous revolutionary Chi Guevara, so we thought it would be exciting to visit there. A fortnight in the sun with some interesting tours was just what we needed.

We had to get flights from Belfast to London and then take an eleven and a half hour flight to Cuba all in one day. We had been up so early in the morning that it seemed like we had been awake for twenty four hours by the time we arrived at the luxurious hotel in Varadero.

We were very tired and then we were told that the hotel couldn't accommodate us all on the same floor as we requested when booking. John and I would have been happy with whatever rooms they allocated but Elizabeth and Daniel insisted the rooms had to be close to each other. The receptionist gave the keys to a porter and spoke in Spanish. He beckoned us to follow him and went out into the grounds of the hotel. We couldn't believe it when he opened the door of a lovely villa with a wraparound balcony. It had views of the sea, pool, tennis courts and jacuzzis as well as the beautiful gardens. Inside there were two large en suite bedrooms, a sitting room, a kitchen and a bathroom. The porter asked, "Is this ok for you?" We didn't hesitate in accepting the wonderful villa that would be our home for the next two weeks. Our booking was all inclusive, so our meals were served in the hotel. After breakfast next morning we could hardly wait to see what the beach was like.

It was more beautiful than we could ever have imagined. The sea was azure blue and the beach of fine white sand was fringed by palm trees. It was a shell seekers paradise. We had been warned not to take the large conch shells as they would be taken from us at the airport. Elizabeth and I collected a few of the small shells to remind us of our holiday.

A short walk across the beach was a little bar where we had a light lunch and cool drinks. We avoided the dessert buffet as the sparrow-like birds seemed to favour it. As we sat there we discussed the many trips that were available and selected which ones we would take.

We decided that a trip to Havana was a must. We had seen it on television before going to Cuba but nothing prepared us for the trip back in time. The buildings were so old they were positively crumbling and I thought a few gallons of paint would not have gone amiss but somehow the deterioration added to the atmosphere. The classic cars were reminiscent of a time of grandeur, whilst delicious aromas came from the little fast food shops at street level.

Starting at Capitol Building, our guide took us on a walking tour of the different squares. We were told about the history and we took time to admire the architecture. We visited a square with a lot of book stalls and local artists came up beside us and drew caricatures which they gave us for a little money.

The squares were alive with the rhythm of music and dance and the culture of happy people. Their smiles and laughter were evident everywhere we went and I thought we could do with having a bit of the same atmosphere at home to brighten up the dull winter days. There were characters dotted around — big women wearing colourful long dresses and turbans and smoking fat cigars. Some of them were toothless. They could have been men dressed up for photographic opportunities for the tourists.

We had photographs taken with the wall mural of

Cuba's most famous revolutionary, Che Guevara. A visit to the market selling art left us in awe of the pictures — the colours were so vibrant. Also for sale were wooden carvings of animals and Cuban cars. Before leaving we visited a cigar factory. It was fascinating to watch the cigars being made while the aroma of tobacco leaf was all around us. Cuban cigars are known as the finest in the world and although they are expensive, we bought some to take home.

Back at the hotel we had a swim and dressed in cool summer clothes, had dinner and enjoyed the entertainment that was on outdoors every night of our holiday. The staff were friendly, the waiters smartly dressed in black and white, the waitresses with long legs, short skirts and pretty faces. On one of our trips the guide told us that the people of Cuba are highly educated. A lot of people had qualified as doctors, teachers, lawyers, etc. yet they were working in menial jobs because they couldn't get work in their own professions. Our guide had qualified as a pharmacist.

We spent some time relaxing on the beach as the winter sun was our main reason for going to Cuba, but I always felt a little guilty as well. It would have been nice to take everyone we knew away from the cold grey days of winter at home and let them have a couple of weeks to bask in the sun as we were doing.

One day Daniel complained his ear was sore. It looked red and swollen. He saw a doctor and was told that he had been bitten by a sand fly. The doctor was concerned he would end up with a cauliflower ear. He was given medication, told to stay out of the sun and not to have alcohol. This was not exactly what he wanted to hear on an all-inclusive holiday.

Feeling sorry for himself, he positioned his lounger under the parasol and informed me he was to have cold compresses put on his ear every fifteen minutes to bring down the swelling. Keen to have him well, I proceeded to run up and down to the sea, soaking a flannel in the salt water for his poor ear. After doing this several times I looked for him and he was on his way to the bar for a beer with John. Well, I decided I would not be attending to him anymore!

He was conscious of the size of his ear and how red it was, and he joked he would soon be able to wind surf with it! Thankfully it was okay in a few days.

We took a two day trip to Hemmingway's Marina. The author, Ernest Hemmingway, spent much of his time in Cuba and he is well remembered there. While we were in Havana we had been taken to a little bar where he used to drink his favourite Mojitos; we were unable to sample them as the bar was too crowded, but we enjoyed them in the peace and tranquillity of the hotel later. We moved into the hotel at Hemmingway's Marina for two nights stay and the yachts did not disappoint. Their beauty and opulence made me aware of how the other half live and this was not something I expected to be reminded of in a communist republic. John was impressed enough to want to take a photograph to show to a friend who is a boating enthusiast at home, but immediately a crew member appeared and asked him not to.

Our reason for this trip had been to go to the famous Cabaret Tropicana. The show is outdoors and the dancers are among the best in the world. The costumes were amazing and at one point the dancers even had many tiered candelabras on their heads. We had got dressed up for dinner and the show and our table was close to the stage. The handsome waiters carrying trays of food and drinks aloft, attended us all evening. At one point they even left a bottle of Havana Club Rum on the table with Diet Coca Cola so that we could mix our own drinks. These are known as Cuba Libras and may have been the reason we slept so well that night despite being in a strange place.

There was so much to see and do in Cuba. One day we took a tour into the countryside and after a motorboat ride across a lake, visited a crocodile farm. Although we had lunch there, I did not sample the crocodile meat on offer but everyone that did said it tasted like chicken!

We had a visit to a coffee plantation and also to a little island on a lake where there were tepees of Cuban Indians, (as they were introduced to us then, but perhaps they are more properly called indigenous people.) It was an unusual experience as the Taino danced around us purifying the air with branches of leaves. They also put black streaks under our eyes before allowing us to enter the largest of the tepees. It was interesting to see the fire lit inside and the smoke being drawn up through a hole at the top of the tepee.

We also had a visit to the Bay of Pigs, a location in the south-west of Cuba that is associated with an event from my childhood – the failed landing operation in 1961 of those in opposition to the Marxist Revolution. It was hard to believe that I was on holiday there, swimming in one of the local pools surrounded by the peace, on a sunny afternoon.

By far one of the most exciting trips was a ride through the Mangrove Swamps. We were on the leading jet-ski and Daniel was told off by the organisers for going too fast. He wasn't too happy about it, but I was delighted as I was clinging on to him frightened for my life. You would have thought he was eighteen instead of fifty. It must have reminded him of his motorcycling days when he was young.

Elizabeth and John thought the ride on the jet skis was really exhilarating too.

When we approached the little jetty I set one foot on it and the boat started drifting away from it! It was only with the help of others pulling me in that I narrowly escaped going into the water. We were then taken to a mini zoo where a baby crocodile was being passed around and a snake was being draped across people's shoulders, a sense of panic arose in me and I couldn't wait to return to the coach and journey back to the hotel.

The Cuban experience had been fascinating. It was a country that had so much to offer and yet here again was an extreme gap between rich and poor. Knowing this, we had not taken jewellery of any great value with us except our watches and wedding rings. Elizabeth had accidently left her watch in the bathroom at the hotel and it had disappeared. When we were leaving we gathered up all the medicines and pharmaceutical supplies we had with us and Daniel gave them to the doctor who had treated his ear. Drugs being in short supply because of the embargo with America, the doctor received them gratefully.

We returned home with beautiful suntans — the others would tell you I only ever look golden and don't tan as well as they do. Despite the many trips, I was well rested and ready to resume the 6am rises to serve my own guests.

Unlike our trip to The Gambia, our holiday in Cuba had been the height of luxury. I realised that it was only because we were staying in the row of luxury hotels in Varadero, travelling by luxury coach everywhere we went. Most Cubans did not experience this side of life and again I was reminded of how fortunate I was. We were working hard at home but we were being well rewarded financially for it. Although the Cubans were working hard I knew it was not the same for them. I found myself thinking about the "have" and "have nots" in these countries and I wondered why the wealth could not be more evenly distributed. I remembered my father saying, "the world is badly divided" and suddenly I knew what he meant.

Work took over our lives again, that and trying to have a family life amidst all the comings and goings of a busy Bed and Breakfast.

I had been doing country house accommodation for tourists for eight years. I loved meeting people from all over the world, and each year brought new challenges and life was never dull. The work was hard —and often I was so tired that I was glad when bedtime came. It had been interesting and mostly fun, and it gave us a little bit extra for luxuries on top of Daniels's salary.

After a period of having five contractors from

England staying for a few months I was feeling exhausted. They had booked in for bed, breakfast, packed lunches and evening meal, and I was expected to do their washing. The work seemed never ending when Daniel came home one day to tell me of an exciting proposition. His company was offering voluntary redundancy — with a good package — for its employees. He was fifty years old. Should he take early retirement? Laughing, I said, "Take it, we will sell this place and move to Tenerife."

We had been to Tenerife on holiday four times, and we loved it. Before we knew what was happening we had booked a trip to view property. We spent two weeks looking around with agents and didn't see anywhere suitable; our money would only stretch to an apartment or a semi-detached house — not the lovely villa in its own grounds that I had imagined. We quickly reached the conclusion that we might get a better property for our money in mainland Spain and returned home feeling a little disheartened. The climate in Tenerife would have been ideal — neither too hot in summer nor too cold in winter.

We came home and put our house up for sale. It was large with five bedrooms and it took a few months to sell. During this time, the contractors remained with us and we also had to accommodate people wanting appointments to view the house.

The work continued to be hard after the break in Tenerife. I knew that moving was the right decision.

There was also the business of finding a new house in Northern Ireland.

Our eldest son, Alan, who was twenty-five, had moved out but Gary, our youngest son of twenty-three was still at home. We talked to him and decided we would buy a house together. He would live in it and we would have a place for holidays or to move back to if things didn't work out in Spain.

Everything worked out well in the end. A local restauranteur bought the house — complete with guests — and we found the perfect property to buy with our son in the same area.

There was to be a month in between leaving one house and moving into the other, we could put our furniture in storage but where could we go for a month?

Homeless In Hawaii

During the time the house had been up for sale I phoned Elizabeth one day and told her about a wonderful holiday I had seen advertised. "It would be the holiday of a lifetime," I said, just as I had described the previous two when we asked them to go with us. "There are three weeks for the price of two. Wouldn't it be great to get some winter sun?" I don't know why I gave her the hard sell; Elizabeth was always ready for a sunshine holiday. When I told her our destination was Hawaii she said, "I've always wanted to go there."

However, John was a little bit more reluctant. "Sure we have had a couple of good holidays and anyway I wouldn't be going for three weeks." I imagined he was thinking about leaving his business and the preparations he would need to make before going. The three of us began to coax him. We told him we might never get the chance again and anyway we wouldn't be going for another couple of months. We said it would be beautiful, just like the Elvis Presley film *Blue Hawaii*. I explained that Hawaii is made up of a group of islands and the one we were going to was Oahu. We could take a trip to Pearl Harbour. We could sunbathe on the famous Waikiki Beach. The conversation went on and on, and before we left John had become as enthusiastic as the rest of us. He didn't give us a firm yes that night but he and Elizabeth did soon after.

Between booking the holiday to Hawaii and setting off for the airport, a lot happened. Our house had finally been sold. We had to vacate it a month before taking possession of the one we were moving to. My sister said we could stay in her house for a few nights as she would be on holiday at that time and we managed to book our holiday to Hawaii for the other three weeks.

We stayed with John and Elizabeth the night before flying to London. We had to be at the airport early and besides we were homeless. In just over three weeks' time we would have our new house.

We flew from Belfast to London and after spending a bit of time at the airport we flew to Los Angeles, although we only saw it from the air. It wasn't the best time to be going to America as we were travelling in November 2001 and the world was still reeling from the terrible tragedy of 9/11. Security at the airport was tight, and there was a feeling of tension all around.

The last flight was to our final destination, Oahu.

While we were getting settled into our seats on the plane, we heard a commotion behind us. Two security officers held a prisoner in chains; he was bound hand and foot. It was discomforting to see this. They asked a small American man to move so they could all sit together. He said, "No, I am not moving." We looked at each other in shock. He said, "I have paid for this seat, I am not moving and I know my rights." I couldn't believe it! The group of three had to find seating together further back on the plane. The prisoner sat between the two men with a blanket over his head for the rest of the flight. I was relieved when we landed in Oahu.

As we were going through the airport, we had the traditional welcome of flower garlands placed around our necks by beautiful girls and it felt like we had arrived.

We were taken by coach to the hotel, which was in Honolulu and just a short walk from Waikiki Beach.

The hotel was pretty average; it looked out over high rise apartment blocks on one side and the main street on the other. Unlike Cuba where our initial rooms had been far apart, this time we couldn't have been closer to John and Elizabeth as our rooms were actually adjoining, but I was far from happy with the tiny and cramped accommodation.

Elizabeth and John offered to swap, as their room

was marginally bigger, but that didn't sit well with me. They told us to ask for another room, but I was too tired as not only had we been travelling a long distance, but we had just packed up our belongings from our previous house. In the end, due mainly to me being physically and emotionally exhausted, I decided the room would do. We all agreed we would knock if we were using the interconnecting door. At least we had our own bathroom, so that was something to be thankful for.

We also had the meeting with "Auntie Mary," the tour guide, to look forward to in the morning.

As we sat around waiting for the meeting to begin with tea, coffee and cupcakes, an English couple beside us announced to those who were listening that they were not happy with the hotel and that they knew their rights. Later they told us they were being moved to another hotel. Perhaps I should learn from the people who stand up for themselves when I travel, I thought, but at that point in time moving felt like hard work and besides we might not have been located anywhere near John and Elizabeth.

Before leaving Northern Ireland, Elizabeth told us that a couple they had met and became friendly with on a previous holiday would be staying at our hotel. Elizabeth had talked to the woman on the phone and she insisted she and her husband would come too.

We met John and Elizabeth's friends at the hotel in Hawaii and they seemed friendly. He was from Scotland and she was from Ireland. We all had a few drinks in John and Elizabeth's room. Next night they invited us all to their room for drinks before dinner. They were smokers, as were John and Elizabeth, and I remember thinking it was such a smoky atmosphere I couldn't possibly have them back to our room.

What puzzled me was the fact that they had not been married long but they lived in two different countries. They explained that every time they met up for holidays, it was like another honeymoon. It was a second marriage for both of them and since they each had children they didn't want to uproot them, so they just continued living in their own countries. Strange setup but it seemed to work for them!

Elizabeth, John, Daniel and I always had an arrangement where we split up during the day time, unless we were going on a trip. Sometimes we would be on the same beach, but in different areas. One day our sun loungers were not far from theirs when a Japanese film company came up to us and asked Daniel and me if they could interview us for television. We said yes, but I was in such a state. I can't remember much about the interview, I was so busy fixing my hair at the time. We had a laugh with the others about it later.

In the beginning we had gone to Waikiki Beach together. It was much smaller than we had expected and, quite frankly, after the beach in Cuba, we were disappointed. Looking at what I saw before me was nothing like the beach in the Elvis film. I hadn't expected the hula dancers but I did expect it to be more like paradise. It was busy with water sports, banana boat rides, outrider canoe rides and, of course, surfing. As we entered the beach area, John was asked, "Going surfing big guy?" We teased him about this for the rest of the holiday. The price of the sunbeds was extortionate at $10 each per day, considering this was back in 2001. We paid for them but the others didn't and I didn't blame them. I just felt we hadn't travelled all that way to lie on the sand. Elizabeth and John alternated between Waikiki and another beach with their friends.

After a few days Elizabeth found the pressure of being with two couples and trying to keep everyone happy too much. She wanted to spend some time with John.

Daniel and I decided we would go to the most expensive restaurant in the area that night. It was a restaurant with a revolving floor, so that we could enjoy the wonderful views. At the beginning of the evening I went to the bathroom before dinner and when I came out, the floor had moved and I couldn't find my table. I was shown back to it by a very efficient waiter. I don't suppose I was the only diner that had ever happened to.

I had been used to silver service when travelling on board ships with Daniel, but I felt intimidated by the amount of cutlery on the table. There were at least seven sets of knives, forks and spoons of all shapes and sizes. I had always known to start at the outside and work my way in, but what if I wasn't having all seven courses? After a glass of wine, I told myself to relax and enjoy the meal — I would never be there again, so what did it matter? After that we had a lovely night. The food was exquisite.

The six of us were looking forward to Thanksgiving. Having seen big American family dinners on TV we were perhaps expecting too much. We had booked a nice restaurant and got dressed up and we were quite surprised when everyone seemed to be in casual clothes. You would have thought they would have made an effort. The meal was okay, but didn't compare with the homely Thanksgiving dinners we had seen on TV.

Young men in military uniforms were asked for ID to make sure they were 21 before they were served a beer. It seemed strange to me that they were considered old enough to fight and perhaps die for their country but they couldn't have a beer until the age of 21.

I had grown up in a home where alcohol was frowned upon. Alcohol was enjoyed in moderation in our own home and I hoped our boys would remember that in our absence. They had both been allowed a beer since the age of sixteen and we had never had a problem with them but I know that is not always the case where alcohol is concerned.

Sometimes we sunbathed by the pool at the hotel, but the chatter was so loud we didn't do it very often. The lunches by the poolside were good and consisted of delicious multi-layered sandwiches. The men usually ordered what sounded like a 'picture' of beer, but was of course a pitcher.

One afternoon strolling through the market I happened to notice a sign for a clairvoyant. I was not a young girl wanting to know if I would meet a tall, dark handsome man, I had already met him! However something told me I needed to visit her and surprisingly she was able to see me without an appointment. She was small and slender with fair hair, perhaps in her sixties; what my grandmother would have described as 'ringle eyed.' I once asked what she meant by this and she explained it meant someone with no colour to the iris of their eye. It was the first time I had met someone like this and I couldn't help staring. In fact I was so busy gazing at her face that what she said caught me completely by surprise. She told me I had brought a well-dressed, educated man with me. He was in Spirit and he looked after me as if I was his own daughter. She said I was never to be afraid if I felt his presence. Believe it or not it was a great comfort to me. I had sensed someone sitting on the edge of the bed from time to time and I had secretly been worried sick about it. I stopped worrying the moment she told me and I was glad I had gone to see her.

It was usual for us to take an excursion every few days and one of our trips was to Pearl Harbour National Memorial. The weather was absolutely beautiful and there was a feeling of peace and reverence for all who were lost when Pearl Harbour was bombed by the Japanese on that Sunday morning in 1941. We were taken by boat to the site of the sunken Arizona. You could have heard a pin drop as we stood there watching the colourful little fish swimming around the wreck of it. We were able to go on board the USS Missouri, best remembered as the site of the surrender of the Empire of Japan, which ended World War Two.

We took a coach tour one day and not only was our guide very knowledgeable but he had a great sense of humour too. I don't recall all the places we visited but one of them was the Dole pineapple plantation. Until that moment I thought pineapples grew on trees, so I was surprised to see them growing on plants on the ground. We also visited the famous

North Shore, where we spent some time on the beach. Our guide told us never to turn our back on the sea because it is unpredictable. Watching the surfers was mesmerising as they rode in on the crest of big breakers. I wondered if they were brave, mad or stupid to tackle those waves.

Travelling around the island, I was in awe of the beautiful tropical scenery; the stunning mountains, sea views and palm trees looked even more spectacular in the setting sun.

We went to the Polynesian Culture Centre one day to see a pageant called Breath of Life. It was set on the river and we had cool drinks as we watched the floats representing the different Polynesian Islands. The people on them were dressed in grass skirts and they danced to the incredibly beautiful music. This was the Hawaii we had wanted to see and it was just like the movie.

Although I was expecting Hawaiian people to live as modern Americans in sky rise apartments in the cities, I think I had a romantic notion of what life would be like on the rest of the Island. Now such scenes are reserved for tourists as theatrical spectacles. I suppose those who visit Ireland feel the same sense of disappointment as they seek out old lime washed cottages like my grandmothers, which now sits in ruin.

The other couple didn't stay with us for the full

three weeks and I was glad, we were happy to have John and Elizabeth to ourselves again. I suppose our holidays were as much about spending time with them as they were about the destination. We had some fun together after we were on 'our own' again.

One night we had arrived back from the beach and had a couple of drinks in their room. We then decided that instead of getting dressed up to go out for dinner, Daniel and John could go out and bring us some takeaway food from one of the many fast food places. They arrived back with filled rolls and crisps, something we hadn't asked for. We asked why they hadn't brought what we sent them for and they told us they were scared to cross the busy road after having a few drinks. We laughed so much that we couldn't be angry with them.

One afternoon, while we were in our room, a young man knocked the door. As he walked through our room, he explained that he had forgotten his room key and his friends weren't in. He proceeded to climb over from our balcony to his, even though we were quite high up. We later discovered the police were watching the man's room as they suspected him of having drugs. Talk about innocents abroad— we had been either very naïve or too trusting of strangers. Since we had travelled extensively I assume it was the latter.

Honolulu hosted a Band Parade one afternoon,

which was billed as the largest in the world. It was obvious they had never heard of the Twelfth of July parades in Northern Ireland. Living in a Catholic area as a child we didn't put up a flag at the 'Twelfth' and I didn't go to see the parades until I was in my early teens. I went with my friend but my father and mother sometimes took the younger children to see the bands returning to the town at 6pm, by that time the bandsmen and women were tired from marching, playing instruments and carrying the Lambeg drum or the banners associated with each Orange Lodge. Once back on home ground they managed to put on a good show for the people who had come out to see them. While the Americans twirl the baton, in Northern Ireland we know it as throwing the band stick. Children as young as three or four practice it coming up to the Twelfth and for a week or two after. As you can imagine by the time they are grown up they are experts in their field. When someone leading a band is really good at this the crowd love to watch them perform. Although lovely to watch, the parade in Honolulu would not have compared to the number of bands we were used to at home.

We assembled outside the hotel early on the morning of our departure to await the coach to the airport. John pointed out a few ladies of the night to us, I looked at the wall with a beautiful spiritual mandala painted on it. It was a reminder of the diversity and contrast of the island we were about to leave.

I wondered if I was being fair in my assessment of Hawaii. Our hotel had been changed days before going and I had been disappointed to find the hotel we were taken to was similar to a concrete apartment block in the town and our room had been such a let-down. We had paid a lot of money for the holiday and I had expected better. I had felt anything but glamorous after the house move and if I am honest I hadn't wanted the other couple joining us. I wondered what my mother would have said if she had known the thoughts of her daughter, the little girl who had come from such humble beginnings complaining about Elvis's beautiful Hawaii. I think she would have reminded me of a saying we have in Northern Ireland, "Never jump out of the bowl you were baked in."

Apart from that, the tours with humorous, knowledgeable guides had been superb. The scenery on those tours had been stunning and the people we came into contact with had been warm and friendly. Although Waikiki Beach had not been as peaceful as I had hoped I had spent most of the time on my sun lounger on one of the best known beaches in the world planning where I would place the furniture in our new home. Perhaps the island of Maui or one of the other islands would have been better suited to my needs? Oahu had certainly been another experience and I was learning that on a spiritual level we all need experiences in order to grow. These are life lessons. I had gone through a range of emotions especially at the Pearl Harbour Memorial, those emotions help us to empathise with others. What a beautiful part of the world it had been in which to learn those life lessons.

The Great Adventure

Perhaps part of the frustration of Waikiki Beach was that I was without roots; I knew I needed to set up our home before going to Spain.

After our holiday, we stayed with friends for two nights and the following day our furniture was delivered to the new house. On the day we were to flit, it rained out of the heavens and our lovely antique furniture had to be dried off with towels as soon as it was brought into the house.

It was good to have a base again. We slept better that night than we had in a while.

Although the house had a beautiful en suite bedroom, which would have been ideal for us when we came home to Northern Ireland for holidays, we decided our son deserved it more. He was making his first big financial commitment and he would be living there permanently. We chose another bedroom and Daniel fitted a range of built-in wardrobes to store our clothes and some of our belongings. For a time, I was busy and happy unpacking and preparing the house for Christmas, but in my heart, I knew this was a temporary home and already I thought of it as my son's house — a lovely, four-bedroom house with a big garden in a village outside Larne. It was a good area and I knew I would be content leaving him there and besides, he loved the place.

Did I feel guilty about leaving our boys? No, they were both in long-term relationships and had good, well-paid jobs. Our eldest son Alan, had his own business in property management and Gary our youngest son was a Project Manager. They could come to Spain for holidays often and we would always come home to Northern Ireland every Christmas and at least one other time each year to see them. There were no long tearful farewells.

I saw my parents before leaving, I don't think my father realised we could be living in Spain for some time since we had booked return tickets for two weeks' time. My mother said, "I'll miss your stories." She didn't say she would miss me! She had arthritis and didn't go out much so she loved hearing about the world and all that was happening, through me. (Later we went on to write to each other and I loved getting her letters with news of home. Our roles had been reversed and I was the one waiting for news.)

Almost as soon as the Christmas decorations were packed away, we booked an apartment in Spain for two weeks and boarded the plane for sunnier climes.

We were ready for our Great Spanish Adventure.

We had arrived in Alicante Airport to beautiful weather, similar to our spring at home. It was good to see blue skies and sunshine after leaving dull days and low temperatures.

As I stepped down from the plane, I realised we had our new life ahead of us. The world, as they say, was our oyster.

We got the tour bus to Benidorm to the apartment we would stay in for the next two weeks, from which we would spend our days viewing properties in search of the one that would become our new home.

Never having been to mainland Spain before, I took in every detail on our journey from the airport. I was fascinated by the pale hillsides along the motorway, the wide expanse of the tolls, the long tunnel, the black metal bull sculptures, road signs of unknown places and places I only knew by name. Now and again there were little houses with orange or lemon groves. I marvelled at the abundance of fruit on the trees. Sometimes there was the odd graffiti covered derelict house, made empty by the progress of the motorway, no doubt.

As we approached Benidorm, I was amazed by its scale. I had seen photographs of it in tourist magazines, but they had not prepared me for the sheer size of it.

After the winter weather we had experienced at home, it would have been tempting to spend our days on the beach and sightseeing. However, we were there for a reason and there would be plenty of time for that later on.

One Sunday, we decided to take the day off and walk along the promenade at Benidorm's Levante beach. I couldn't understand why the people were dressed so differently. The younger British people were wearing swimwear, the older British pensioners were dressed in track-suits and the Spanish wore fur coats! I remember saying to Daniel, "Who has got it right?"

A couple of days later, we hired a car and headed south to Torrevieja.

We had seen adverts for a company who were flying people out from the UK and showing them property in that area. We decided we would make an appointment with their representative to be shown around.

Nothing could have prepared us for the number of houses there.

Halfway through the day I admitted, "This is not what I had in mind." The agent asked me what was wrong. I explained that I needed space around me, that perhaps I would be better living in the country-side. He looked perplexed and said, "But this house has a nice blue roof." I thanked him for his time and we headed back to Benidorm. Although it was a big city with high-rise buildings, I knew there were beautiful quiet areas along the coast from it; we were soon to find out that they came with a much higher price tag than the properties in Torrevieja.

We spent a little time finding agents and booking appointments. I will never forget the first *finca* or country house we went to see. An old couple had lived there; the old man had passed away and the old lady lived close by with her brother. The brother came with the agent to show us around. The ornately carved wooden bed almost filled the small bedroom and above it was a large picture of the couple on their wedding day. I could have cried when I saw it. The bathroom, kitchen and sitting room were still furnished. It looked as if the owners had just stepped outside. It had a *deposito* of water that might have passed for a swimming pool and an orange grove. The old lady's brother gave us an orange each; they were warm from the sun — the most beautiful oranges we ever had.

The finca was too small for us but the view down the valley to the sea was breath-taking. We stood looking down over other little white fincas and fruit trees, some under netting to protect them from the wind in winter, and I thought that we would have felt blessed to live there.

Next we were taken to a semi-detached villa. The

agent told us the houses had been built by two brothers, but they couldn't get on together and one was
selling. From that day on, we called it *The Brothers'
House.* As we passed the first house to get to the second, the dogs started barking ferociously and this
continued throughout the viewing. It put us off buying the property, which was a pity as the house was
full of beautiful features inside —wonderful Castel-
lan doors, a carved wooden staircase and terracotta
and cream marble tiled floors throughout. I loved it.

The viewing of a little finca followed. The driveway was flanked by two huge, very old, gnarled olive
trees. I don't know what I expected, but the house
was tiny. The young man who lived there had taken
in a lot of stray dogs and he was so kind that he was
feeding them out of his own money. He was in the
process of renovating the house to sell. Again it was
much too small for us.

I was learning that behind every home lay the
story of its people.

A different agent took us to see a new finca, built
about eight months before we arrived. It was owned
by a young Spanish couple. The house was perfect at
first sight. The lane, which served quite a few houses,
was one kilometre long and rough. If only we could
have lifted this house and set it near the sea, which
was about twenty minutes' drive from it, but then it
would have been out of our price range. Daniel had

asked the owner if he could video our tour of it and that night we talked of how we would furnish it and add a pool on the spacious site. We compared every house we looked at with the finca at the end of the long lane after that.

Our days were speeding by, with some viewings in the mornings and some in the afternoons. We met with a new agent and he took us north to see two properties in Gata de Gorgas.

One was beautiful, in need of a bit of work, but the noise from the motorway in the distance put us off buying. The other property was like cattle sheds ready for conversion. Both properties unsuitable and the drive back to Benidorm was as hair-raising as it was on the way there. The agent admitted he had been a rally driver many years earlier, which explained why he was cutting off the bends and driving on the wrong side of the road more often than not.

We met up with the rally driver one more time near the end of our two weeks and he took us to see a beautiful property near a village. The house, built on one level, was in its own grounds and it had a pool and sea views. It was exactly the kind of place we had in mind when we decided to live in Spain. We were unable to see the inside as the owner was in Holland, but we fell in love with it. We told the agent we had to go back to N. Ireland for a week and asked him not to sell it to anyone else. In the meantime, he was to get the keys so we could view it when we returned.

Our thoughts were on little else when we went home to see the boys. We were excited on the journey back thinking that the villa would be our new home. Sadly we were missing my father's seventieth birthday. When I left his present and his birthday card I placed the best photograph I had of myself in it, I wanted to feel that I was with him even if it was only in Spirit.

On our return to Spain we contacted the agent, the property had been sold by a joint agency.

We rented an apartment in the same building as last time for one week, later moving to another one for a month, and despite our disappointment we resumed our search for our new home straight away. This time with another agent.

He took us to see a new-build villa in a village, but the noise of dogs barking reverberated all around us. It was no to that one.

Next came an older villa with a steep drop behind it, and we discovered there was a dry riverbed at the bottom of it. They can remain dry for years and suddenly become flooded and overflow. You would have thought this was reason enough not to buy but the agent added, "The man next door keeps bears, but if they are too noisy he will take some of the bigger ones elsewhere." I looked at him in amazement. Seeing this he said, "Come, I will show you."

At the back of the other property were a few aviaries of birds.

I explained to him what we were expecting to see and the three of us had a good laugh.

Another property had a big crack in the driveway, with a steep drop to one side. Yet another had a large crack in the wall of the house. The land it was built on was too soft and it was beginning to sink. We were told we could remove the land around it and infill with concrete, but we decided not to take the risk.

There are few things I am uncomfortable with, but one of them is snakes. I don't mind them in the wild but I wouldn't wish to be too close to them. An agent took us to see a building site with superb sea views. It was overgrown. I asked nervously, "Would you get many snakes here?" He replied, "Yes, this is the *campo* — the country. They only come out when it is very warm, don't worry about the big long ones — they are okay. Look out for the little short ones — they are vipers. Very dangerous!" We no longer had plans to build there, despite the wonderful views.

We had been living in the residential apartment block for almost a month. Families went about their daily lives, coming and going at all hours of the night. To say it was noisy is an understatement. The ground floor was a restaurant and we could hear people working at three in the morning. They were chopping vegetables and preparing the food for the day. We were not sleeping well and despite looking at a few more properties we had not found anything to compare with the little finca with the one kilometre lane we had seen near the beginning of our search. It was becoming more attractive with every passing moment.

A thought came to us both at the same time. We could buy it and have all the peace and quiet we wanted. We would have a great sleep and begin to feel human again. It would be bliss to live a little further away from people and, besides, we could buy our own car instead of the rentals we had been using. It was only five minutes' drive from the village, where we could dine in one of the many little Spanish bars. We could have long lunches with tapas in the afternoon. We had been told there were quite a few English families there so we could make friends.

It was then we realised we could make it work — the new life, I mean.

We had a second viewing the next day and we were right; we hadn't seen anything that compared to the little finca among the pine trees. We put our offer to the agent and within a fortnight the sale had gone through. We were moving in.

We had been so busy since we had started the house hunt. We had a Spanish solicitor who spoke English, NIE numbers required by the Spanish Government and we had joined the Community of Owners. We had opened a bank account and set up a direct debit to Iberdrola, the electricity company. All of these things had taken a lot of time; we were proud of what we had achieved.

Moving Into The Little Finca

It was with relief and excitement that we moved in after getting the keys. We had bought a few essentials as soon as our offer was accepted and now it was time for the fun of making a home to begin.

We found a big furniture store and its accommodating German owner would have done anything to help us. Most of our furnishings came from his store. Mattresses came in different grades and he told us, "Buy grade one for your bed but grade four is plenty good enough for guests." When buying pillows elsewhere we were told the same about them. We laughed so much as we had always given the guests the best in the house.

The master suite had a bedroom, large bathroom and — for the first time in our lives — we had a dressing room. We bought a beautiful polished wooden bed frame, chest of drawers with matching mirror and bedside cabinets for our room, and pine furniture for the two guest rooms. We found a large oak table, six chairs and a matching dresser style cabinet for the dining area and a cream leather corner suite for the sitting room. A TV and cabinet, coffee table and collection of mirrors and pictures completed the interior, not forgetting the beautiful floor standing wine rack for the wine we intended to consume over the coming year.

We had arrived with just two suitcases of clothes and while some might say that was very liberating, I felt a bit bereft of all my belongings. We had made friends with the people who owned the Irish Bar near the apartment we had rented and I was so grateful when the owner gave me a Guinness tea towel for our new home. I had a greater sense of appreciation than before. The German owner of the furniture store gave us a hamper of luxury foods. It is the kindness of strangers and the little things that matter when you are away from family and friends.

There is so much to find out when you move to a new country — practical everyday things, like which of the post boxes belongs to you. You need to understand the recycling system for the bins at the end of the lane. Canisters of gas were subsidised by the Spanish Government and therefore quite cheap. They had to be collected from a lorry parked in a layby. It made sense to use gas for the heaters and also for cooking, although we had an electric oven.

Electricity was limited to three kilowatts, but after installing the air conditioning and swimming pool, this had to be upgraded to eight kilowatts.

Suma was a tax that had to be paid for the rates on the property and also for the car.

Water was ordered by telephone and arrived by the tanker load, costing sixty Euros. It was pumped into the *deposito* which was a large storage tank in the ground. Drinking water was bought in bottles from the supermarket or collected from the village font. It was fresh spring water and usually our preferred option.

We paid for private medical care on a yearly basis. We had occasion to need it one morning when Daniel woke with the white of his eye completely red. We went to one of the clinics in Benidorm and within thirty minutes he had seen a consultant and an eye specialist. It was a burst blood vessel and nothing serious. However, we were impressed by the way he was treated.

During our time in Spain I went for the usual female appointments. When I visited the gynaecologist he shook hands with Daniel, bowed and kissed my hand and after my examination sent me for a mammogram, giving me the results there and then and I walked out with the x-rays in my hand. I was stunned; after all, I was used to waiting a fortnight for my GP to give me the information I needed in Northern Ireland.

February turned to March and we had put a home together quickly, which was just as well because John and Edna, a couple of friends from Northern Ireland were coming to stay with us for a holiday. We thought it would be a good time to have a house warming. Any excuse for a party!

We had a party for ten, even though we had only moved in a few weeks before. I was surprised because we hadn't known a soul when we arrived. Daniel's cousin Hazel, her husband Ivor and son-in-law Norman came over to stay in their holiday home in Torrevieja. They travelled up for our party and stayed overnight.

We had invited our friends from the Irish Bar, who were also from Northern Ireland, and, by coincidence, they knew our guests. It was such a fun night and the little finca was well and truly warmed with love, laughter, jokes and music. The food was good and, having cooked far too much, we had enough for the following day. The house felt more like a home after that; it was the start of a long list of friends visiting and having parties. We settled in very quickly.

We made many friends in the village and we were never lonely.

Dining out was reasonably priced, which meant we went out for dinner about four times a week. All Spanish restaurants offered *Menu del Dia*, which was a three-course meal with wine for just a few euros. I remember going into a restaurant one night and the owner came to take our order. There was no written menu and she quickly told us what was on offer in Spanish. Seeing that I had not understood, she took me by the arm and pulled me into the kitchen, stirring pots and opening fridges and drawers, laughing all the while. I chose dinner and it was very good, but I made up my mind I would always be able to order a meal in Spanish. I never had the same problem again.

**

Once we had settled into the little finca for a couple of weeks, the next step was to buy a car. We had been renting since we arrived, and while it was cheaper than it would have been in the UK, we knew that we needed a car of our own.

Buying a car was not an easy matter, and Daniel and I were not on the same page as far as it was concerned. I wanted a sturdy four-by-four for the rough lane and wasted no time asking the dealers for a *quarto et quarto*.

Luckily they didn't bring me eight cars to view!

Second hand four-by-fours were as rare as hen's teeth. They must have been part of the dream for everyone. We almost bought one until we discovered it would only do twenty miles to a gallon of fuel. Second-hand cars, in general, were expensive.

Daniel fancied a white van with windows. He said

there would be enough room to transport the cases of the many visitors we were expecting. Now, at home the 'fish man' had a wee white van and he delivered fish around the houses once a week. I just could not see us in a wee white van.

We viewed many cars, even ones I knew on sight were not for us. One day we went to an open-air car sales place. We thought we might find one there until the young salesman lifted a car bonnet; there were lots of empty nut shells around the engine. When Daniel enquired about them the salesman said rats ate them at night and also chewed the wires sometimes. We couldn't wait to get out of there.

Eventually Daniel had the idea of going to the car hire company since they changed their cars on a regular basis. From there, we bought a dark blue hatchback. It would suit our purpose and look stylish enough at the same time.

Getting insurance for it was a new experience. When you go into a Spanish office to conduct business, the person you are meeting gets to their feet and warmly shakes hands while giving you eye contact and wishing you a good morning or evening. We explained what we wanted and after taking our details, he looked at me and said in all seriousness, "When you have an accident, you will be very nervous, don't be nervous, as you must fill in this form." He went on to explain the procedure. He needn't have bothered. Even though I had driven in the UK for thirty years, with only a minor scratch on the car during frost, I never drove in Spain.

Daniel and I had a good laugh after we left the office. Thankfully he took to driving in Spain like a duck to water. Once we had the car, we were ready for visitors from the UK.

Each new arrival elicited excitement. After the finca and pool had been cleaned, we would pick them up at Alicante Airport and Daniel would give them the tour on the way to our house. He would point out the local landmarks. His patter never varied very much and guests would affectionately call him *the tour guide*. They got a tour of the little finca when they arrived and they were pleased to have exclusive use of a shower room.

None of our friends or family had a pool at home, so it was a novelty with children and adults alike. One spring we had taken the cover off the pool after winter and we told our guests that it was a bit cold to swim in at only eighteen degrees. They pointed out that that was the same temperature as the pool in the Leisure Centre at home. It was apparent that we had acclimatised to the temperatures in Spain.

The adults loved lounging in the pool with plastic glasses of Cava, while the children helped themselves to ice lollies and ice creams from the well-stocked freezer in the casita, the little house behind the main house. Our one rule was that if we went out sightseeing during the day, we stayed in at night, and vice versa.

We lived about twenty minutes' drive from five pretty seaside towns, so there was always plenty to see and do. Most of our visitors loved to walk up through the narrow winding streets of the old Spanish village, and afterwards we all sat outside the little bars and people-watched with a cool drink.

Sometimes we went to Calpe and had a trip on a glass-bottomed boat, before dining on freshly caught fish at one of the little restaurants by the harbour.

The Algar Waterfalls was another favourite. It was possible to swim in the cold, crystal clear water, a welcome cool down in the heat of the day.

Guadalest is a beautiful old village perched high on a cliff in the hills, looking down on a turquoise lake to one side and pine clad valleys to the other — a tourist's dream. It is also a shopper's paradise, with the most wonderful shops lining the little streets without taking away from the age and character of the place. There, all tastes are catered for — Lladro China, fine glassware, embroidered linens, paintings, leather handbags, exquisite jewellery, beautiful things for the home and also cheap trinkets reminiscent of a holiday in Spain.

Little museums are interwoven into village life in Guadalest. There is a Doll's House museum, the Salt and Pepper Pot museum and the Torture Museum. The Museum of Small Things features unique items like a painting carved on a grain of rice. There is also an ancient tower, a lovely old chapel and a gaol in the village.

A drive to Albir and Altea in the morning sunshine before it got too hot was always popular. We would walk past lovely marinas and beaches and perhaps visit the Crystal Shop. Lunch would be a wonderful salad and crusty bread or sometimes a Chinese meal — an inexpensive and appetising choice.

We usually avoided Benidorm in July and August, what with so many people and the difficulty of finding a parking space, but when we had people staying we sometimes took them there so that they could sample the amazing nightlife. The children enjoyed the go karting and the Terra Mittica theme park was a great day out for all. We would tend not to join the families on their trips to the Water Park.

The best nights, everyone agreed, were those when we stayed at home. Daniel barbequed chicken and other meats and I prepared salads. We ate outside on the terrace, the reflection of candle light dancing on the glasses and bottles of wine until the wee small hours. Our chat and laughter rang in the still air, which was scented by a mixture of Jasmine and the Citronella candles to keep the insects at bay.

I remember being a little hungover at breakfast one morning when our friends Gordon and Eleanor were staying and Gordon said, "She who hoots with the owl at night shall not soar with the eagle in the morning." It was a saying I never forgot.

Cats And Geckos

When we bought the little finca, the young owners asked us if we would like to keep their two German Shepherd dogs. We had to say no because we were planning to go to Northern Ireland for three weeks occasionally and putting them into kennels would not have felt right. Also we did not know how they would react to the many visitors we were expecting for holidays.

However, we did end up with a new addition to the family. Their cat Paco had gone missing when they were leaving, and they said if he turned up we could keep him; they were moving to an apartment. As we said our goodbyes to them they warned us that Paco didn't like to be picked up.

We didn't have long to wait for his arrival. We looked out and he was sitting on an old table at the back of the house, where he normally had his food. He was a large tabby cat — grey with black stripes — and when he looked at us we felt he was as wary of us as we were of him. I watched Daniel as he kept his distance while setting the food down. Each day he moved a little bit closer and the whole scene reminded me of the film 'Dances with Wolves.' Every day the pair of them eyed each other while building trust and eventually Daniel was able to stroke him. He would say it was one of his greatest memories of our time in Spain.

Paco became my friend and soon he got himself a girlfriend. He proudly brought her to meet me one day and I was not impressed! Apart from the fact she was not a nice looking cat, she had a sneaky way about her. We called her Matilda. We didn't want a lot of kittens arriving and every time we saw her we chased her. She was in love with our Paco and she would not be put off. She came back again and again to see him.

One night I decided to have a bath. This was very rare for me because we normally had showers, the water being paid for by the tanker load. As I lowered myself into the luxurious bubble bath, I heard the distinct sound of kittens. They couldn't possibly be in the bathroom, I thought. Yet they seemed so close. I finished bathing and, wrapping myself in a towelling robe, I went to the sitting room to tell Daniel what I had heard.

The next day, he crawled underneath the house, where there was a gap for the convenience of installing plumbing and electricity. He heard the sound but couldn't see the kittens. The noise was coming from directly under the bath. Placing the video camera up the hole beside the waste pipe he saw the kittens; Matilda had crawled up there and had them in a safe place.

Daniel came out smiling and said to me, "They must have thought they had central heating last night with the heat of the bath." On a more serious note, he told me they would not be staying. As soon as they were old enough he would take them to the cat sanctuary. He watched Matilda coming and going until one day she took a dead mouse in for the kittens. He realised they were ready for solid food and guess what? He bought cat food with the groceries and put little plates in there every day.

One day after rain Matilda brought the kittens out to introduce them to the world. They came out, lifting each little paw and shaking the rain off. We fell in love with them.

Matilda turned out to be the most wonderful mother to her kittens. We spent hours watching her train them. She taught them to climb an old stone wall by standing at the top and calling to them, encouraging them all the time. She did the same when it was time for them to climb the pine trees.

I had dug over a little area in the garden, intending to plant herbs, but Matilda had other ideas. She decided it would be the perfect place for toilet training her kittens! I allowed them to have it and I was rewarded by them never using any other place in the garden.

Something I was not so pleased about was when they took the heads from my succulent plants to use for hunting practice. They played with them outside our bedroom window at first light. It sounded as if they were having a game of football.

They were growing fast into three beautiful tom cats and I was sad about that. I knew that one day Paco would no longer tolerate them being there. He would chase them as he did every other tom cat that dared come on to his property. Although he was friendly towards us, he remained quite feral.

Sometimes we would hear terrible screeching and see the shaking of a pine tree and we would know that Paco was fighting with a strange cat at the top of it. One day he came home with part of his nose missing. We were never sure whether a cat or a snake had been the cause of it.

We would also see little geckos (small lizards) in the garden and one night Daniel came in and told me Paco had caught one. I said, "It is ok, they shed their tails to fool their prey while they get away." He looked at me sadly and said, "Paco wasn't fooled."

Thinking of geckos reminds me of one time when I was cleaning the bathroom. A movement in the bath caught my eye. I watched in amazement as my bikini top moved along the bottom of the bath. Suddenly a gecko appeared from under it and left the house by the bathroom window, which I suppose was the way he came in. I was so relieved that it wasn't a snake.

A friend explained that geckos live in family groups and he would have loved them to live in his apartment to catch any mosquitos and flies that came in.

Like all wild life, I preferred them to stay outside. Even our beautiful cats had been trained to stay out of the house. All four sat in a row on the kitchen doorstep waiting expectantly while Daniel dissected a cooked chicken from the supermarket, Carrefour. How they knew we had bought one with the groceries, I will never know. They seemed to appear each time we bought chicken.

Leaving Spain

It was a few weeks before my fiftieth birthday. Daniel and I had been living in Spain for three years. I stood at the gate and looked at our little finca, our country house, painted yellow with white balustrades. It looked lovely in the sun.

Our four cats were in residence, two of them draped over the couch on the terrace, the others at the rear of the house.

Sunlight sparkled on the swimming pool and the scene set among the pine trees was a joy to behold. Within our boundary, I had counted twenty-seven pine trees; it was an offence to cut down a pine tree and this law was policed by the people from the Town Hall. The valley and surrounding hillsides remained green.

Daniel and I were so happy there. We had lived and laughed and loved like two newlyweds playing house. We had made so many new friends. And, now, sadly, we would be leaving them behind. It would be good to see our old friends and our family in Northern Ireland. They would miss the wonderful holidays they had shared with us in the warmth of the sun.

I looked at the garden we had created. It had many climbers around the perimeter fence. The soil had been so hard we had to use a mattock to dig holes to plant the Honeysuckle, Plumbago, Bougainville, Solanum and Jasmine.

We had been told that the Spanish usually plant Jasmine near their gate for a perfumed entrance. Returning from the village on those warm sultry nights, we could understand why. The fragrance was heady and delightful.

Massive terracotta pots of pelargoniums filled the spaces along the fence. Red geraniums filled the window sills and we had to replace them often because of the geranium moth, which seemed to drill little holes in the stems. We didn't use sprays. It was just as easy to replace the geraniums when we knew visitors were coming.

The flower beds were U-shaped and surrounded by stones. They contained a variety of shrubs and plants. My brother-in-law had jokingly called them my weed beds. It was true that they had not flourished quite as well as I had hoped. Water was not plentiful; we had to buy it by the tanker load and it was used sparingly for the plants, so we saved the dishwashing water to supplement it.

We had, what we grandly called the orchard. It had a few young fruit trees — lemon, orange and nisperos, which are about the size of a plum and the colour of an apricot when ripe. They were sweet and perfect for bottling. The day we brought the trees home in our estate car the perfume was so sweet and intense. We had such high hopes for them. Together with a few other small trees they did not an orchard make. However, they were precious to us.

The orchard was bordered by the young plants of what was to become a lantana hedge. We chose it because it had flowers like pompoms in red and yellow, which gave it the name Spanish Flag. One day Daniel found a massive blue and yellow caterpillar eating the leaves. It was eating them so quickly we called it the Munchkin. When he showed it to our Belgian neighbours, they insisted they would keep it as they would like to see it pupate. They asked us for Lantana leaves to feed it. The first time Daniel obliged them, but then laughingly told them that they would have to get them elsewhere as the Munchkin was eating so many.

**

Swimming in the early evening was heavenly, the water was wonderful after the heat of the day. The Mediterranean diet and living closely with nature agreed with us. Not only did we feel healthy, but we had an all year round suntan, so we looked healthy as well. Having a swimming pool meant we swam several times every day between April and early October. In summer, the heat built up over the course of the day, and the hills beyond our fence had a pungent aroma of pine trees and wild rosemary, lavender and thyme. There was a strawberry tree on the plot below ours. I was like a child studying it with wonder the first time I saw it.

Chilling out with a glass of Cava, we laughed and talked about the day's events and our poor attempts at speaking Spanish. We had an understanding of it if it was spoken slowly, but the Spanish evening class we had gone to before we arrived hadn't left us with the confidence to hold conversations of any length. Still we got by on it and, thankfully, there were quite a few English speaking families in the village.

Our neighbours were wonderful. There was a little Spanish family who came to welcome us home after we had returned from a trip to Ireland. We looked out and they were standing at the gate in their pyjamas. They were generous to us, even though they knew we did not speak a lot of Spanish.

We visited a couple in a big house further down the lane. The man was American and his wife was Norwegian. We spent many a happy evening with them on their terrace, while the red wine flowed and

CDs of jazz piano filled the warm evening air. Supper was always cheese and crackers —simple, yet satisfying.

We loved those evenings when we walked up the rough lane — slightly drunk — hand-in-hand, listening to the frogs on the plot below.

Soon the adventure would come to an end. No more would we watch the eagles soar overhead in the mornings as we had breakfast alfresco on the terrace. (We dined lightly on orange juice, cereal, fruit and tea). No more would I watch my husband Daniel happily cleaning the pool after breakfast in his turquoise shorts, his body brown from the sun

**

Business and shopping were conducted in the morning before it got too hot.

Often we had coffee outside one of the little bars before returning home. I ordered café con leche, coffee with milk and Daniel ordered cappuccino. Almost always the waiters would mix them up and give me the frothy creamy confection.

Lunch was salad, melon and ham, tomato, mozzarella and basil and *pan* with aioli. The rest of the ingredients varied but there was always crusty bread and garlic mayonnaise — the preventative against the mosquitos biting. Yes, after being there for a while it worked.

In summer I spent the siesta in the pool lying on an air bed reading my book. One day I noticed a wasp drinking the droplets of water from my legs. I remained very still as it flew away and returned many times.

Our neighbour kept bees at their home in Belgium. He told us that bees take water back and blow it into the hive to cool it in hot weather. He asked how I knew it was the same wasp. I told him it was wearing a striped jumper! He said he would love to bring his bees to Spain, I asked how he would transport them and he said, "I will put them in the car and tell them they are going on their holidays." I thought bees would have been perfect there because of the wild lavender and rosemary — the honey would have been good — although, I would never have been brave enough to keep them.

After swimming in the afternoon, we hung our wet towels over the balustrade of our little finca, bringing even more colour to it. The heat didn't seem to bother Daniel and sometimes he would work through the siesta. I always rested between two and four in the afternoon — when in Spain, do as the Spanish do!

Sometimes I would lie dozing in the hammock we had strung between two pine trees. I swung gently and listened to the bells clanging in the distance. The sound coming from a herd of goats further up the mountain was oddly comforting. All was well until one day a shower of ants descended over me along with some pine needles; it was not so easy to get out of a hammock quickly, I discovered.

Daniel thought it was hilarious the day I insisted he phone the electricity company about the noise from the pylon on the hillside. The humming noise was coming from cicadas in the trees. I don't think I will ever be allowed to forget that one.

We had enjoyed showing our home off to family and friends when they visited. It had three bedrooms, two bathrooms, a dressing room, a lounge/diner, spacious hall and an empty room in which we had installed our choice of kitchen. For a month we had to make do with a two burner gas stove, and luckily there was a sink unit installed.

By the time we got our kitchen delivered, we appreciated it. We chose beautiful light oak units and Spanish Marble (granite) worktops. The kitchen had been pre-tiled, as is usual in Spain. We had been promised the kitchen on Easter Tuesday morning, and when it didn't arrive Daniel phoned the shop. He was told that the lorry should be with us. He walked down the lane and discovered the lorry with two men asleep in the cab. The lorry couldn't make it up our muddy lane as it had rained for two days. The delivery men were waiting for someone to tow them up to the house. I thought this wasn't a good start for the new kitchen, but I needn't have worried — they had the units and appliances fitted in an afternoon. The Spanish Marble was then delivered and fitted in another afternoon. It was perfection. I had forgotten that kitchens and bathrooms are something the Spanish do well. It takes at least a week to fit a kitchen in the UK.

We were especially proud of the porch, which ran the full length of the house. We had designed it ourselves and instructed the builders as to how we wanted it. The work had taken much longer than we were told to expect, and, at times, we were sorry it had been started. When it was finished we were delighted with it.

The covered terrace had archways and wide steps leading up to the front door. It had space for an extending table and chairs to seat twelve at one side and a settee and coffee table at the other. The settee had been left behind by the young couple who had sold us the Finca; it was extremely comfortable and looked quite chic with a blue and white checked throw over it.

Someone had left a television and video player at the *basuras* (bins) at the end of our lane. They had been kind enough to stick a piece of paper with the word *funcionada* (it works) to the screen. We took it up to the house and put it on the terrace. Visitors appreciated being outside with the rest of us, yet able to stay in the shade and watch TV when it was too hot. We had benefited from the Spanish way of recycling.

One man's trash is another man's treasure.

With some beautiful big plants in blue, glazed pots at the corners and plates on the walls, our terrace looked wonderful. We had placed outdoor tables amongst the trees so visitors could have a bit of space when they stayed. We also had what we called the Shirley Valentine table with one chair. If someone sat there it meant they wanted some time alone. It wasn't used very often.

At the rear of the property was a *casita* or little house; we used it for storage, but the young couple had lived in it while the house was being built. It had a shower, WC and wash hand basin. It came in handy as a changing room for swimming. It also contained a second fridge for cool drinks.

I knew there would be tears the day I had to leave here. I also knew there would be days in the future when I would wish I was back.

I don't know what it is about the properties we live in, but it takes such a long time to sell them. It is as if they don't want us to leave. That was how it was with the little finca also.

Once we made the decision to go home after being there just under three years, we went back to the same agent who had sold us the property. The sale was well advertised and we kept the house and gardens immaculate for viewings. We had a lot of viewers, but it took nine months to find a buyer. People would complement us on the presentation and the décor, but we wouldn't hear from them again. It seemed like such a long time since we had made the decision to go home to our boys. Both of their relationships had broken up and they were living together. I felt they needed us. Maybe I was feeling a little bit of guilt about leaving them after all.

At this point I began feeling unwell. Assuming it was stress-related, I went to see a doctor.

He told me my blood pressure was high and put me on medication. After a few weeks, I didn't seem to be getting any better. Someone recommended a Healer called Kenny and I went to see him. It was obvious when I met him that he was someone very special. He had such presence and the kindness and compassion in his eyes told me I could trust this man with my life.

He asked for my hands and after taking them he said, "You do not know why you are feeling like this? You are a healer. It is because you are not using the healing energy and it is building up in your body that you are feeling unwell." My hands had felt very hot for some time and sometimes they tingled. I also seemed to be able to tune in to how others were feeling. Complete strangers would tell me their problems. It was clear to me that he was right. We spent two hours together. Kenny channelled Spiritual Healing to me and I felt calm for the first time in a long time. I told him of our delay in selling the house, and, smiling, he told me it would be sold within three weeks. Kenny was a Medium. He had many gifts, Healing was one and clairvoyance was another. I asked if he would help me by showing me how to use the healing energy, and I promised I would see him on a weekly basis until I returned to Northern Ireland.

Just when we were getting tired of the viewings, friends told us they knew a couple who might be interested. They asked for a suitable time to bring their friends to do a viewing. Once more the little finca was looking its best. The viewers came, but didn't seem enthusiastic.

Within a couple of weeks, however, they got in touch with an offer for the full asking price, which we accepted.

Knowing how quickly things moved when buying the property, we knew we would only have a short time to organise everything before going back to Northern Ireland.

We couldn't have found a nicer couple to buy the little finca. The man had a business in the area and he was keen to make everything as easy as possible for us. They asked if they could buy our furniture, and not knowing if it would be a good fit for a future home, we sold it to them. The house we had bought with our son in Northern Ireland was already furnished. It was our intention to live there until we sorted our finances out and found a house of our own.

Even though the couple bought the furniture, there were so many other things we wanted to take home — pictures, mirrors, urns, bedding, clothing, kitchen equipment and our lovely wine rack, of course. We had about forty boxes of personal effects and Daniel organised a lorry from the U.K. to take everything back for us. Ours was to be a part load on a rather large lorry that was too big to come up the lane.

The future owner said he would send up a small lorry to take everything down to his business; he would also store it until it was collected. He gave us boxes, bubble wrap and tape to pack it all.

When we said we would need somewhere to stay for two weeks until we were due to go home he said, "No problem, you can stay in the apartment I own in the village." We had never met anyone so kind and decent in all our house transactions and we couldn't believe our luck.

Now we had to make plans for our beloved cats and there was no question of them going home. Apart from anything else, the lifestyle at home would not have suited them. My heart was breaking at the thoughts of them going into a cat sanctuary; they had never been caged and I couldn't bear the thoughts of leaving them in one.

Our new friend said, "No problem, they can stay with us. We will be happy to have them." What a relief! We would always remember them in the setting of the little finca. They would be there long after we had gone.

I think the scene I am about to describe will stay with me forever. Daniel was at the back of the house, in front of the casita constructing packing cases from wood to support our beautiful Spanish urns. Cardboard boxes lay strewn around the white gravel. I stood at the back door watching our beloved cats playing in and out of them as Paco lay looking disinterested on the old table where he had his food. I had to turn away to stop the tears from falling.

Everything went according to plan with our boxes of personal effects. How on Earth had the couple who arrived with two suitcases accumulated all this stuff in three years? Our suitcases were packed, and, despite my sadness at leaving, I smiled when I looked at them.

Someone had once said to us, "You might have arrived with two suitcases, but they must have been full of euros."

On the morning of the house sale, we got dressed

to go to the Notary. We took time to walk around the property, each of us deep in our own thoughts. I was grateful that we had sold the house after so many months. Mentally I thanked the little finca for keeping us safe and being a happy little home for two people getting to know a new country, culture and language.

We went to the Notary's office, met our solicitor and the others and conducted our business in much the same way as we had when we bought the property — only this time the money would be going into our bank account instead of out.

Afterwards we treated the new owners to lunch in an expensive hotel.

We then agreed that we would wait in the little finca until they brought their things from the apartment we were about to stay in. We left wine and cava in the fridge for them. It was evening when they returned.

Daniel showed the new owner how everything worked, and I helped his wife to bring their clothes from their car and hang them in what had been our dressing room — the one I had been so proud of when we arrived. It was their property now and we wished them every happiness in their new home. I genuinely hoped they would be as happy there as we were.

We took a last look around as we told them the

cats had been fed. As we passed the swimming pool on our way to the car, I remember thinking I will probably never have one of those again. We were driving out the gate for the final time and I thought of how many people dream of moving to the sun and how few make it happen. We had done it! We would never sit in a nursing home when we were old and wish we had made the move.

We were still in our early fifties, still young. In two weeks' time a new chapter in our lives would begin with all the excitement it would bring. We had to come to Spain for me to find out I was a healer. What would I do with that news when we returned to Northern Ireland? Daniel sat in the car beside me and I asked him how he felt. He said, "You know me, I could be happy anywhere." It would be good to see our boys, but we would never regret the time we spent in Spain in the little finca among the pine trees in the sun.

A Time To Heal

We returned from Spain to find our two handsome sons waiting for us at the airport. It was a wonderful reunion and we were all happy to see each other. During the days that followed I told our boys what the healer had told me. They took the news really well and they didn't seem surprised by it. They were supportive just as their father had been.

After a few days I realised my boys didn't need me at all. They were men, used to looking after themselves. They were having a ball and both of them were in new relationships. We offered to buy our youngest son's share of the house so he could find somewhere else. He told us he loved the house and didn't want to move. He suggested he would buy our share and we could find a house of our own.

We began looking for a new home, one we might settle in for a while. We chose the nearest large town which was Larne, so we could be close to our family. Having looked at a couple of properties, we selected a beautiful bungalow with a large garden; it was backed by trees and surrounded by large shrubs and hedges. (Coincidently, the couple we bought the bungalow from had bought it on their return from Spain.)

Once again it was fun making a home, but it was also tiring. We had new windows installed and we painted all the doors white. I think most people like to put their own stamp on a house. It was beginning to feel like home.

My father and mother had divorced many years earlier and each lived with their new partners about ten minutes from us, and quite a few of my siblings lived even closer, so we had plenty of people always popping in to see us. Since we had lived far away from them for three years it was lovely to see them when they called.

We had a little greenhouse at the new house and I planted lots of bedding plants for the garden. We were content and not long after we came home Daniel's old firm telephoned to ask him to come back to work on a temporary project. He was happy to return to work after the long rest in Spain.

I wasn't home very long when I decided I needed to do something about the conversation I had had with the healer before leaving Spain. He had said that I too was a healer and he had given me some training in Spiritual Healing. Now this wonderful man was so far away and I was alone with this knowledge. He had told me he would only ever be a phone call away but it wasn't the same. Daniel was supportive, but didn't know what my next step should be.

I had believed in God all my life; I couldn't remember a time when I hadn't. Therefore, I didn't see myself as a 'Born Again Christian'. I wasn't professing to have found the truth, I had always known it. I was in no doubt that a greater power than us exists. Each day I followed a little routine when I got up and before I went to bed. I prayed for protection from negative energy. I asked God to surround me with His Divine Light and make me a good channel for His healing. I asked Christ to be the Light on my path and I asked forgiveness for my sins. I didn't know what else I could do, and so I continued to pray. I started reading the Bible and those words that had seemed strange to me before, made sense to me.

A strange thing happened. A calmness came over me and I found myself meditating. For a week Jesus came to me during the meditation. He descended a white staircase and I was in awe of this amazing energy that quickened my heart. There was a sense of wonder and the most incredible feeling of Love.

He appeared as I have seen Him in pictures. Each day he was dressed in robes of white, blue or red. He held out a gift to me which I received. I felt humble. I was so overcome with the whole experience that I found myself shaking. I cannot say what he gave to me. I know that if I talk about the experience, it will be spoiled. After this, I talked to Christian friends. I needed to know if this had happened to them. I didn't go into detail, and it was just as well. The first person said, "The devil can also heal."

A family member looked at me as if I was pathetic when I told her I had been chosen to be a healer. "Why would God choose you?" she asked. I should have said, "Why would he not?" Instead I became upset. What if she was right? Perhaps she was wondering why He hadn't chosen her, as she was a 'Born Again Christian'. I allowed doubts to set in, even after the proof I had been given of the presence of Jesus Christ in my life.

I told another friend who talked me into speaking to a Presbyterian minister. A visit was organised for me. As the time for the meeting approached, I began to feel nervous. I prepared a tea tray and asked Daniel to bring it in when we had talked for about fifteen minutes.

The minister came, and I talked while he listened. I told him of my meditation experience and I knew by his puzzled expression that the same thing hadn't happened to him. He was kind. He told me to be calm and that God could heal without me. There was no hurry.

This was not what I wanted to hear because I wanted to start using this amazing gift. I was so nervous that I had forgotten to pour the tea and he had ended up pouring it for us. At the time I was embarrassed about this but later when I thought about it I found it funny. I should have been the one to say, "More tea vicar?" but it had been the other way round.

A few days later he called unexpectedly to ask if I would like to accompany him to a healing service. I would have loved to, but I had promised an elderly friend I would take him out for lunch and I didn't want to disappoint him. I thanked the minister for inviting me to the healing service but explained I had other arrangements. Later I sent him a little card of appreciation for all his help. That was the last I heard from him.

Alone again with my thoughts, I read in the local paper of a woman who had been ill and had a miraculous recovery by using Reiki Healing. I phoned her and discovered she was about to offer Reiki Courses. Since I would be able to learn about the different hand positions used in healing, I asked her if I could come along. She said yes and I felt I was no longer alone. I did my first and second degrees in Reiki and later I became a Reiki Master. I enjoyed being in a Reiki group. Together we would send healing to where it was needed. The group also sent healing to individuals and gave healing to each other.

It was through the Reiki group I heard about Angel Awareness evenings and most of the others also went along too. Attending those evenings about once a month for three years, I discovered that we can all connect with Angels through meditation. I had some of the most wonderful experiences of my life during that time. The world is a beautiful place when you allow yourself to be divinely guided. I also learned that Angels cannot interfere with our free will until we ask for help. This was something that I and probably many others did not realise. Angels are always available to us.

People will read this and ask —is she crazy or is she some kind of saint? The answer is neither; I am an ordinary woman, and if it happened to me, it can happen to anyone. Healing is something we are all capable of — from the mother who comforts her baby to someone holding out their hand to a friend in distress. Healing is something we do instinctively.

I loved partying in Spain but as soon as I was told I was a healer, I stopped drinking spirits. However, I decided life would change too much for us as a couple if I gave up alcohol completely. There would be no harm in a glass of wine now and again.

Did I become a Christian overnight? If a Christian is someone who believes in Christ, then that is what I am, but if it means going around and telling people they must drop their own beliefs and religion and convert to Christianity, then the answer is no. I have come to believe that if someone has respect for a Higher Power, his fellow man and the flora and fauna of the Earth that is good enough for me. I once heard the saying, "There are many paths up the mountain, but they all lead to the same place." That is my belief also.

I saw changes in myself; I was kinder and more tolerant of others. I was less judgemental, realising that life can be tough and we are all on the same journey but maybe at different levels. I appreciated the beauty of nature more and colours became brighter and more vivid.

I worked on the new house and as I improved it, I also improved my inner self. My thoughts drifted to a better world — the realisation that we are connected to each other and to all things. The Earth is our home and we must learn to share it. It is somewhere we can experience peace and love and help each other through good times and bad. Yes, I was changing and so were my interests, which now included Healing, Angels, Crystals, Prayers and Meditation.

However, I didn't go around preaching to others; I was still shocked by what had happened to me.

It was about nine months later that I saw a counselling course advertised. I felt it would be perfect for me. If people came to me for Reiki they could talk about their problems in confidence and in a safe space. I learned that the best thing I could do was to listen without interruption or judgement.

One course followed another for the next three years and, before I knew it, I had completed my Advanced Diploma in Counselling. As part of the diploma, I had to have ten hours counselling myself and during these sessions I came to recognise how beneficial counselling can be. I met some lovely people and I learned that we all have problems — how we deal with them is what separates us.

During this time, life did not stand still. Although I was not a Roman Catholic, I wished I could go into a convent to escape everyday life and have peace with my thoughts on this path my life had taken. I also knew that this would not be the answer for me as I needed to face up to life's challenges in order to grow spiritually. I needed time to understand all that was happening in meditation and in my dreams. I needed answers from the Higher Source I called God.

I saw a Crystal Course advertised in the Isle of Man and felt drawn to it. Daniel couldn't have been more supportive and he booked the course for me. It was unlike me to travel alone but when I got to my destination, I felt at home. The others on the course were just like me! I fitted in with them like a piece in a jigsaw puzzle. It was where I was meant to be. The facilitator taught us about the energy of crystals and how they can be used for healing. We practised using them for healing each other, moving on to setting up beautiful crystal grids to heal the Earth and the Planets.

It was an amazing time and I was glad to have been a part of it. The lady who taught the course and I developed a friendship which will last for the rest of our lives and hopefully beyond. By the time I came home I knew her well enough to be able to turn to her when things weren't going so well in my life. There are times when healers need healing, because they are sensitive they pick up on the emotions of others and quite often they can tell what illness a person has just by being near them. In the beginning I found myself overwhelmed by all of this. Finding myself like this one Christmas I phoned my teacher from the Crystal Course for advice and immediately she said, "I want you and your husband to come to my home and spend New Year with my husband and me and I will give you healing and look after you." That is exactly what she did, her kindness was beyond words.

It is my belief that we can only try to do the best we can while we are on the Earth. Being kind is a good place to start. Gratitude for all we have and all we are, eventually brings happiness. Love changes people for the better. We must begin by loving ourselves and then we can pass love on to others. Love, ultimately, is the answer to everything.

Grandchildren

I fell in love with my first grandson as soon as I saw him.

I wasn't one of those women who pines to be a grandmother. I had been the eldest of seven children and I had helped a lot as they were growing up. I had also brought up two children of my own, so there was no yearning for babies. It was not long after we came home from Spain that our eldest son, Alan, got himself a house near his business and his girlfriend Jill moved in with him. One evening they told us they had some news for us. We were to become grand-parents. I took each day as it came, prayed the mother and baby would be alright and knew Daniel was looking forward to becoming a grandfather.

When our grandson arrived he wasn't an easy baby, but his father hadn't been either in the begin-ning. Alan hadn't slept a whole night until he was nine months old. As I held my new little grandson against my left shoulder, the way I had held my own sons, I knew we had bonded.

I realise that everyone thinks their grandchildren

are the best, but he was such a clever little boy. We had a holiday in Tenerife with him and his parents when he was about eighteen months old. He wanted to run around the swimming pool constantly, so we put him into the crèche for a little while so we could sunbathe. He wasn't there very long when we were told to come and collect him as he was screwing the bolt off the door! Sadly his other grandmother, Jill's mum, who loved him very much took ill and passed away. We are the only grandparents he has left and we have always been very close. He says he would love to live with us and that says it all.

After four years a little brother came to the Earth to join him. He was the happiest baby I had ever seen — always smiling, always content. He is still bright, funny and clever. I loved him also but he didn't bond with me immediately, in fact he looked past me to see where his grandfather was. When he was about two years old I threw a balloon to him and smiling he threw it back to me. The fun continued for some time and that was when we really bonded.

Another four years passed and a little sister arrived. She is a born entertainer and loves to sing and dance. She puts on fashion shows for us and concerts. We go on holidays with our grandchildren and they visit every Sunday. Sometimes the whole family come for sleepovers. What did we ever do without them?

Our second son, Gary asked his girlfriend Natalie to move in with him shortly after we moved to the bungalow in Larne. In the beginning they had two dogs and three cats and they seemed very happy. Gary then announced his company had head-hunted him for a job in England. The company had made him an offer he couldn't refuse and he, Natalie and their menagerie of animals piled into the car and set off for the South of England. They rented out their house near Larne and, although I was sad to see them go, I couldn't say very much as we had left our family to go to Spain.

We had some wonderful holidays with Gary and Natalie, we flew into Bristol, hired a car and stopped in Glastonbury on the way. I had only seen the festival on TV before, but I loved the little town with its crystal shops, complimentary therapies, second hand book stalls and nice little places to eat. You can visit the Chalice Wells and drink the healing water or take a walk to St. Michaels Tower on top of Glastonbury Tor. It is said to be an area associated with King Arthur. The Michael and Mary Ley Lines run through Glastonbury creating a wonderful energy. I was in my element walking around and Daniel loved it too.

Daniel and I visited Stonehenge and Avebury Stone Circle, and we also enjoyed exploring Dorset. We went to Dorchester and I was reminded that the area was the setting for some of Thomas Hardy's novels. As a young girl I had enjoyed reading them, they contained romance but also character studies that I found fascinating. I was delighted when they serialized *The Mayor of Casterbridge* and *Tess of the D'Urbervilles* on TV. It felt good to be walking in areas that had inspired his writing.

It wasn't very long before two little English grandchildren arrived. First a little boy who looked like his father and, soon after, a little girl who looked like her mother. Even though we only saw them about twice a year, the children came to us on our visits as if we had never been apart. It broke my heart every time we had to leave them and I was glad when my son said he and his partner were returning to Northern Ireland before the children started school.

Gary had sold his house near Larne the previous year, and so house hunting again became part of our lives. While they were still living in England, Gary and Natalie shortlisted a number of houses they had viewed on the internet. We would drive past to view some of them and have appointments for viewing others. Sometimes Gary or Natalie would fly over if we saw something interesting.

Just when we were all getting tired of the viewings, they found the perfect house in a village near Ballyclare which is about thirty minutes' drive from where we live and they have been happy there ever since. The children have a large garden to play in and are seldom indoors. Both of them have settled into their primary school and have friends. They love living near their cousins and see quite a lot of them. Sleepovers with us at holiday times have become popular with them too. Our grandson is a master at building Lego and our granddaughter is a wonderful artist. We do our best to encourage our grandchildren in all the things they love doing. I show the grandchildren the love my Grandmother had shown me and they have the bonus of a grandfather who loves them all very much.

It still surprises me when children are brought up in the same home, in the same way and yet their personalities are completely different. I feel it is important to nurture the little souls who come to the Earth. Allowing them to develop their gifts and talents is so important for their mental health and wellbeing. They will try doing some things and give up, but it is by experimenting that they find the things they love and are good at.

It took some time for our son to find a job but eventually he found one that would challenge him. Natalie works hard looking after the house, the family and the big garden. She also does the decorating and in many ways she reminds me of myself when Daniel was at sea. The difference being, her man comes home to her at night. Seeing them as a family unit reminds me of how much I missed that while my children were growing up.

The Fragrance Of Egypt

We arrived in Luxor in darkness, and as we were taken to our cruise boat, I wondered at the mysterious land we had arrived in; there was an energy about the place that I had never experienced anywhere before.

Daniel had been asked to work for a longer period than we initially thought, and after being there for two years he felt due a well-deserved break. Looking through the Sunday papers, he had spotted an advert for a trip to Egypt. The holiday would begin with a week-long Nile Cruise followed by a restful week's beach holiday in Hurghada beside the Red Sea. It sounded perfect for us.

This time Elizabeth and John weren't going with us. Their children had grown up and they were enjoying family holidays with them and romantic breaks on their own. Besides, they had visited Egypt already.

Now we had arrived and after gazing at Luxor Temple the first thing I noticed was the horses pulling fringed buggies. It was like a scene from the cowboy films I used to watch as a child at the home of my paternal grandmother who lived in the town. (I had always been on the side of the 'Indians' as I didn't think their land should have been taken from them.) I wasn't expecting this form of transport in Egypt.

Along the river Nile the cruise boats were moored and lit up, waiting for the tourists who were keen to see what this land held in store for them. Going aboard our cruise boat, I noticed the thick green luxurious carpet and the shiny brass hand rails on the corridors leading to the cabins. The crew members were smiling, willing to help in whatever way they could. We were made to feel special from the moment we arrived.

We dined in the dining salon and we were allocated a table with six others for the entire trip. Luckily we all got on well from the beginning and we looked forward to the conversation at meal times. The food was delicious, impossible to fault. One night I had chicken pie and the disc of pastry on top was so light you could have blown it away.

We quite often had entertainment after dinner. The dancers always looked so exotic and colourful. We had an exhibition by Whirling Dervishes, whose dancing had a hypnotic effect on me. I wondered if others felt the same.

We had been told at the beginning of the cruise

that we would dress in Egyptian costume one evening and enjoy a banquet. We bought costumes in the markets we visited before realising there was a little shop on the cruise boat. Discovering this I bought another costume from the shop owner and he helped me with my makeup. Once I was dressed, he offered Daniel a hundred thousand camels for me. Daniel refused his offer, explaining that he didn't know what he would do with all those camels! We had a good laugh and I felt like Cleopatra, I had a wonderful night. I also had a great story to tell when we returned home.

Afternoon tea and cake was served on deck at four o'clock and it was such a lovely time of day. We sipped tea and watched the people going about their daily lives on the banks of the Nile. The scenes were almost biblical. People were dressed in long garments with turbans on to protect them from the sun. Their little homes were basic with thatched roofs and they brought their animals to the water's edge. Some of them pottered along the river in small boats. It was a reminder of how necessary the Nile was to their survival, not only in ancient times but also in this day and age. The Nile had been a matter of life or death to the Egyptians. I remembered how necessary the stream that ran through our farmland had been to us and to the animals.

Our days were taken up with trips to see different

Temples and the Valley of the Kings, burial place of the Pharaohs. It seemed surreal to be standing in places we had only heard of or seen on TV. We had guided excursions to the Temples at Karnak, Luxor and Edfu. We visited the Temples of Hatshepsut and Philae, and it was when we were visiting the Temple of Philae that I had a strange experience. We were approaching the island by boat and the most amazing surge of energy went through my body. I sat quietly hoping no one else would notice how taken aback I was by what had happened. A lady beside me began telling me that she had left her husband behind on the cruise boat because he was ill. I mentally sent healing to him and it was only afterwards I realised the two things were connected. That evening I talked to her and her husband was absolutely fine again. I was so pleased that God had healed him. I felt a closer connection with God in Egypt than anywhere else I had been so far.

In The Valley of the Kings, we visited a few of the Tombs of the Pharaohs and the one I was most looking forward to seeing was the Tomb of Tutankhamun. It turned out to be small and a lot less impressive than the others. I felt a sadness that these tombs had been disturbed and their treasures removed, whether it was by tomb robbers or archaeologists.

Our trip also took us to the High Dam at Aswan.

We could have taken an excursion in a hot air balloon over the Valley of the Kings but we decided to go by coach as I wasn't feeling brave enough; and besides, it required a very early start.

We also had a shopping excursion, my favourite stop was at a shop selling essential oils and perfumes. We were taken in and seated on either side of the room in two rows. Tea in little glasses was brought to welcome us and when we were comfortable we were given sheets of paper with the names of the oils and perfumes numbered. This was so that we could order anything we wanted. The exotic fragrances were dabbed on our wrists, backs of hands and arms until we decided which ones we were happy to buy. Money changed hands and we were told they would be delivered to our boat. I must admit I did wonder if this would happen. I needn't have worried, though; the purchases arrived, as promised. The fragrance on the coach as we travelled back to the boat was wonderful and it was almost a pity to have a shower that evening.

All too soon our week on the Nile was up and it was time to transfer to Hurghada for the second week of our holiday.

There was tension in the air as we got into the minibus to travel in convoy for safety. The convoy was there to protect the tourists following a terrorist attack in the past. Noticing a security man in plain clothes with a gun — supposedly concealed — didn't ease my concerns.

However, I prayed and asked Archangel Michael to protect us and then I felt myself relaxing. After that I sat back and had a pleasant journey alongside the canal watching everyone go about their lives. I had the strangest feeling of having been there before. After a while the scenery became barren and desert-like and we had one stop for a comfort break and refreshments. The place we stopped at was neither a village nor a town; it was more like a gathering of mountain people in a market. They seemed poor and we wondered how people could survive there; I vowed that we would give them everything we could do without on the return journey to the airport.

Hurghada was a development by the beach with luxurious hotels, and we were booked into our hotel just in time for dinner. The restaurant was full of tourists, the noise was unbelievable and it was such a contrast to the peace we had been used to on the cruise. I looked at Daniel and said, "I don't know if I can stay here." He said, "We don't have any other option. It only sounds noisy after the peace and quiet we have just left, but you will get used to it." He was right, of course.

We spent the next week in the hotel and at the adjoining beach, and in the end, it was a restful holiday. The gardens on the way to the beach were beautiful with flower covered pergolas over the path and oval beds of orange canna lilies. The sun loungers were wicker and they were surrounded by large wicker screens for privacy.

We had lunch at the beach and it came from a little stall where they made the most delicious gyros (kebabs) and burgers. With a cool drink it was adequate since we had dinner in the evening. Did we have tummy problems? Of course we did, probably with the change of food.

One evening we had a beautiful meal in a restaurant in the grounds of the hotel. We got dressed up and Daniel had seafood while I had parrot fish. It was something different and we enjoyed it very much.

We took a trip one afternoon in a glass bottomed boat, and since the Red Sea is a wonderful place for divers, we were able to enjoy the spectacular underwater vistas and the many shoals of colourful fish from the comfort of the boat.

Travelling back to the airport we were well rested and we were as good as our word, we took a bag of our belongings with us to give to what we called the mountain people.

Egypt had been a land of mystery, a land that in some places looked as though it hadn't changed throughout the centuries. It had stirred up feelings of a bygone time when rulers lived in splendour and died taking riches with them to prepare for the after-life. Their temples had been so well built by the people they are still standing today. The people lived a very simple life as we saw on the banks of the Nile and for most of them that hasn't changed. They say that fragrance brings back memories and I knew the beautiful perfumed oils would do that for me. The men there had smelt strongly of Frankincense one day and we were told it was because it was a Holy Day and I shall always think of Egypt when I smell its sweet fragrance.

In a way, I envied our friends on the cruise boat; it had been their third time in Egypt and I knew it would be our last. There was so much more of the world to see, and I knew I would never return.

Spiritually I had felt uplifted and my dreams had been unusual and more like meditations. Daniel said his were the same. It is my belief that when we travel it is because our energy is needed in those places. I felt pleased that we were facilitators of the healing the Earth needs so much.

Incredible India

Daniel looked at me as if he couldn't believe what I had just said. "I want to spend a year in India," I repeated. He didn't speak immediately and I sensed he was angry at the thought of me leaving him for a year while I went off to meditate in India.

He had been supportive up until now, but I had the feeling I had crossed the line.

Later he said, "I don't want you to go to India for a year but we will both go for a holiday if you like." I didn't argue with him, yet again I found myself giving in for a quiet life. What I really wanted was to get away alone to spend time getting to know who I was, me, not the wife, mother, grandmother, daughter, sister etc. I had no regrets about marrying this lovely man who had been by my side for most of my life but perhaps I had married too young at eighteen and I hadn't taken time to find out who I was? I felt a year in an ashram in India would have allowed me the time to meditate and pray. I wasn't looking for a Shirley Valentine moment!

We studied the holiday brochures together to decide where we would go. There was a trip to Goa, flights to Delhi and a coach tour to Agra to see the Taj Mahal. We reasoned with ourselves that you cannot go to India without seeing the Taj Mahal, even though it would mean flying to Delhi via Mumbai soon after we arrived. We would spend a few days sightseeing and return to Goa for a beach holiday before going home. This would give us a flavour of India and we would be staying in good hotels, so we would be comfortable.

This time we flew to Manchester where we took a flight to Goa. As a surprise Daniel had booked Business Class for us and it was an absolute pleasure to travel. I have never enjoyed a flight more and I wished we could fly that way all the time. No chance — unless we won the lottery! After arriving at the airport we were taken by coach to the hotel in Goa. It was quite luxurious, and I couldn't wait to have a shower. When I reached the bathroom, I changed my mind —there was a gecko! Yes, one of those tiny lizards in the shower. Daniel had to talk me into sharing the shower with it. The heat of the day convinced me that I had to do it and the gecko did not move; I know this because my eyes were firmly fixed on it the whole time!

After a buffet meal we went to bed because we were being picked up early to get our flights to Mumbai and then to New Delhi. Although it is only two hours twenty minutes flying time, we spent a long time at the airport, so we seemed to be travelling for a couple of days at least. Despite our tiredness the coach driver and guide decided we would go straight into the tour of Delhi and New Delhi instead of giving us a comfort break at the hotel. I didn't feel good and by the end of the day I realized it was motion sickness. Despite feeling unwell I was still impressed by the beautiful buildings. The architecture and wealth of the past was a sharp contrast to the poverty in the streets. There was a dustiness and a special light in India that I have never seen anywhere else.

They are good looking people, the men are handsome and the women are incredibly beautiful with their dark hair, dark eyes and golden-brown skin. The people move with grace and they appreciate colour and use it in everything from their clothing to their furniture. A lot of the food is vegetarian and there is such a selection you are spoilt for choice. I wondered if they could attribute their good looks to the healthy diet.

Travelling through Delhi you see all of life. The roads are constantly busy. There is transport of every kind and I was amazed at how much you can load onto a bicycle. I stepped back to allow someone onto the bus before me and a man pushing a bicycle loaded with reams of paper was so close that he unbalanced it and it ended up on the ground. I felt really bad but the bus was leaving and there was nothing I could do about it. I have often thought about that incident since.

There were all kinds of lorries, cars, motorbikes, scooters and even elephants being used to transport people and goods. Cows wander at random through all of this. People walk amongst it, horns honk and although the traffic lanes are supposed to be one way, they are not.

We were sitting in an air conditioned coach with six other people and I looked at a local bus with so many people inside they couldn't have fitted one more in. There were even people clinging to the outside of it. I felt guilty watching them, yet not for one moment would I have changed places with any of them. It was a strange feeling and I asked God what I could do for these people. The answer I got in my mind was, "Send love to them."

Amid all the noise, there was also an oasis of peace and calm to be found. It was serenely beautiful in the gardens of the Mahatma Gandhi Memorial. Little green parakeets flitted around in the peacefulness of the gardens. Everyone moved around quietly and respectfully. The minute we entered the gates of any temple or mosque, we were in a different world from the one outside the gates where everyone was jostling for space. Perhaps the energy within the temples is because of all the prayers being said.

On the first night of our tour we slept in a fabulous hotel room, although I was surprised to see it was decorated in a Japanese theme. I had to make a mental note that the bed was on a raised dias in case I got up during the night.

The following day we set off for Agra and the Taj Mahal. I remembered Princess Diana being photographed looking very demure in front of it and I had wondered what I should wear that morning. I had settled on cream linen trousers and a cream cotton top with a scene in spicy colours on it. It was very hot and I needed to feel comfortable.

When we arrived at the gate there was a group of schoolgirls waiting to go inside. They smiled at us, and waved their little henna tattooed hands. An Indian man and woman approached us. I assumed like us they were full of anticipation to go inside the gate. The woman had difficulty walking. I don't know if the man saw my look of pity but he told her to come and shake hands with me. Her English was perfect but our smiles and eye contact spoke volumes. I felt that God was using me as a channel for healing and I think she may have felt it too. I didn't see her again among the crowd.

After that I couldn't wait to go inside but our

guide kept talking, all the time edging closer to the gate. The wait felt like sweet torture, but later I appreciated the fact we had not rushed inside. Once we were through the gate, what I saw was perfection before my eyes. I felt so emotional I was almost in tears. The Taj Mahal, built in white marble inset with sparkling semi-precious stones — a joy to behold.

The Taj Mahal was built by the Mughal Emperor Shah Jahan as a mausoleum for his favourite wife, Mumtaz Mahal, in the 1600s. It took 20 years and approximately 20,000 workers and 1000 elephants to build it. Imagine a man loving a woman so much that he created the Taj Mahal as her final resting place on Earth. Their love story is one of the greatest love stories ever told and it seemed fitting that Shah Jahan joined her there after his death.

Before the tour we had our photographs professionally taken while sitting on the very seat where Princess Diana sat. Even now craftsmen work with white marble and hand carve flowers and leaves before inserting crystals in patterns in the style of those used in the Taj Mahal. We purchased coasters from them although I didn't need a reminder of our visit; it was something that will remain in my memory and in my heart forever. The feeling of love when I was there was, I am sure, felt by everyone who visits.

We were taken to a shop selling silk rugs of the finest quality. We didn't buy them but we did buy cushion covers and place mats, which I am afraid to use in case someone spoils them. That night as we had our meal we discussed our tour and later as I lay in bed I thought of Shah Jahan and Mumtaz and the fourteen children they had had. Daniel was quiet beside me but when I asked him about the visit he sleepily told me he had been moved by it.

We returned to the hotel we had stayed in when we first arrived in Goa and Daniel asked for a nice room. Thankfully our room was higher up and did not have any uninvited guests like the little gecko. Our meals were quite often served outside on the beautiful lawns. The tables were covered in white linen and had exotic flower arrangements. All was going well until someone told us they had seen a snake in the area during the day. I was a little nervous after that about dining outside, despite wonderful entertainment like the fire eating, but we had lovely barbecues in a paved area under the frangipani trees. Even now as I write this I think of how privileged we were to visit India and stay in such glorious surroundings.

The hotel offered all kinds of beauty treatments and if I had known they were so reasonably priced, I would have visited their beauty salon sooner. While I was having a manicure and my eyebrows threaded, the beautician told me a little about Ayurveda and shortly after, I booked an appointment. Ayurveda is one of the oldest healing systems in the world. It is said to have been developed more than 3000 years ago in India. The traditional Hindu system of medicine is based on balance between mind, body and spirit using diet, yogic breathing and herbs to achieve this.

A doctor assessed me to customise the treatment to my health needs. After taking my details and examining me I was sent for a massage, which was carried out in a grass hut within the grounds of the hotel, it ended with the therapist gently swinging a brass pot of warm oil which she drizzled over my forehead. It was heavenly.

Most days in Goa, we went to the beach where the young waiters would overdo the attention in the hope of getting tips. One young man offered to massage my legs and was quite annoyed when I politely said, "No thanks." He was persistent and Daniel told him if anyone was going to massage madam's legs it would be him. I was pleased he was so protective. Laughing, I told him I would hold him to his promise.

At the beach, we encountered a jeweller — or rather, he encountered us. His shop was close by and we were easily persuaded to visit. We bought dazzling pendants and bracelets with amethyst, topaz and aquamarine crystals for gifts. As if he hadn't been kind enough already, my lovely husband bought me a Star of India pendant. It is a black oval surrounded by tiny diamonds in a silver setting and I knew how Elizabeth Taylor must have felt when Richard Burton gave her that fabulous diamond. My pendant was not as valuable as Elizabeth Taylor's; it was because it was given with love that it meant so much.

India is written in my heart. It is written in indelible ink in a script that reminds me of the little henna painted hands of the children at the Taj Mahal.

I saw poverty, people sleeping in the streets with their babies and people who were almost skeletal with hunger begging for a few coins. I also saw the other side of India, a land of great beauty and romance.

I was glad Daniel had suggested the holiday because I don't think I could have survived there on my own. I continued to pray and send love to India long after I had gone home.

This was to be the last of our big holidays and if I had known what lay ahead I think I might have asked God to stop the clock at that point in time.

Time To Say Goodbye

If my life looks like a bed of roses, it hasn't always been the case. Death is a part of life and I would deny those wonderful people who shared my life if I did not mention them.

Within the space of three years, from 2014 to 2016 I came to know what grief and loss is. Perhaps I shouldn't say loss, since it is my belief that the soul moves on to another dimension when the body dies and we meet the family and friends we once knew on the Earth.

My brother-in-law's passing left my younger sister and her daughters distraught. It is hard when you see the ones you love suffering.

A close friend passed, she was an elderly lady and she had been very good to my family and me when the children were growing up. She and her sister used to take the boys to the swimming pool and then out for lunch. I appreciated the little time I had to myself and the boys felt grown up when they were being treated. After her sister passed away she and I used to go out for lunch together. The boys used to say,

"Where are Thelma and Louise going today?" teasing me and referring to the film of course.

Not long after that my lovely mother-in-law passed; we had been as close as any mother and daughter. I was heart- broken, she was the best friend I ever had. She was the person I turned to when I needed to talk things over. We phoned each other almost every day. After she passed I found it hard helping to clear her clothes and her possessions from her beautiful cottage but it was the last thing I could do for her here on Earth. I still talk to her in my head often.

Our dear friend, Chris, phoned from Spain to say her husband, Dave, had died. The four of us had spent so much time together when we lived there. She had taught ballet and been involved with the theatre for forty years. She had brought a new dimension to my life and I loved her for it. Her husband Dave had been an engineer so he and Daniel had a lot in common, he had a great sense of humour and had us laughing every time we met them. Little did we know when we visited Chris about five months later that she would die before the end of our holiday. They had looked after me one time when I had spent a month in Spain on my own with Daniel visiting at weekends and it was through their care that I had grown so close to them.

I was having difficulty getting over Chris's

passing and I sat down and thought that I really couldn't continue grieving so much, I needed to move on. Mentally I asked her to give me a sign that she was with Dave and she was OK. I was driving my car the following day when two little birds caught my attention. The elegance of their flight enchanted me as they flew closely together and it looked like they were performing a little dance in the air. I was alone in the car and I said aloud, "They look like twin souls." Immediately I knew that Chris had sent me the sign I had asked for and I was able to carry on with my life.

**

My mother passed away in August 2014. Although she had been bedridden with arthritis for years and hadn't been well at various times, she always recovered. She had been diagnosed with dementia about three years before, it affected her memory but she still knew all of us. Daniel and I had just returned from a trip to England when my sister told us mum had pneumonia. Realising how seriously ill she was I joined my stepfather, sisters and brothers where we took it in turn to be by her bedside. We had a few days to say our goodbyes before mum slipped away peacefully. I walked out of her door and there was the most beautiful rainbow I had ever seen, lighting up the morning sky. I was being reminded that she had taken the rainbow bridge to Heaven and that meant she was free of pain at last.

I am sure you are wondering if I ever gave my mother healing. The answer is yes, however healing works on different levels; there can be a complete cure or a partial cure, in that the pain subsides for a time. Healing is always given for the highest and greatest good, so it means that the person may become mentally able to cope with their health issue. If it is the individual's time to pass, the pain may become more bearable for them.

Not long after I found out I was a healer, my mother, who had known God all her life told us she was a Christian. I felt that was a comfort not only to her but to the family also. When my mother left the Earth I felt a part of me had gone with her.

My father and stepmother had been regular visitors at the home of my mother and stepfather for years. This may sound unusual but it made life easy for the family and there were no awkward moments. I admired the way they behaved like adults.

We have a tradition in Northern Ireland where close family and friends carry the coffin part of the way at the funeral. My stepfather asked my father if he would do this along with him. The two men who had loved her walked side by side in their grief.

My stepmother and my mother had been great friends and I knew it saddened her greatly when my mother passed.

All of this took its toll and for years I saved my tears for my meditation room before going to bed at night. My poor Angels must have been tired of me crying, I knew they were there trying to comfort me, but I was inconsolable for a long time.

Slowly but surely everyday life took over and the crying sessions became less frequent. I still have to watch if I am a little bit down that I don't allow the grief from that time to overwhelm me.

I get reminders of each and every one of the people I lost from time to time. It may be a song, an expression on the face of one of the family or someone telling a story. Now I can laugh and remember the good times. I believe that we never forget those who pass on and the terrible grief we feel in the beginning doesn't last forever; our loved ones wouldn't want it to.

Sometimes we all wonder what we did to deserve the bad times in our lives. I am no different to anyone else. When we see someone going through bad times, we say, "The best years of his or her life came first." That was exactly how I felt. When I was studying grief and loss in my counselling course, I had been taught to draw a timeline and fill in all the times of loss in my life and I felt life had been good until the previous three years.

More was to come, my father's wife, my lovely

stepmother, who was the gentlest, kindest person, was diagnosed with dementia. It took a while to realise there was a problem, but, looking back, the signs were there. Although she loved flowers, the bouquets she was given by the family for Mother's Day remained unarranged in a bucket until they died. She started forgetting her handbag. She visited one day wearing two similar shoes but one was black and the other navy blue. One afternoon while my father was having a nap, she went out in the car. He woke to find her gone and the family formed a search party, phoning around and looking for her.

Hours later she turned up at my house and told me she had been badly parked in the town and hadn't known how to move the car. She was diagnosed shortly after that and my father looked after her with the help of carers coming in three times a day. He struggled with the arrangement as he was a private man and it wasn't easy having strangers in the house. He was also an outdoors type, who had always considered housework and making food woman's work. Yet he did his best and the family did what they could to help but eventually he admitted he couldn't cope. We found a very good nursing home for my stepmother. It hurt to see her go, but we all knew she would have better care there than my father was able to give her.

My father was heartbroken that she had to go but

he could see it was for the best. We consoled him with the fact that he could visit her every day. For a time she seemed happy in the nursing home; she had company and loved to watch all that was going on. She was always immaculately dressed and had her hair done every week. Our family knew the right decision had been made about her care and in his heart I think my father knew it too.

Later because of her condition, she was to lose the ability to communicate, but she seemed happy enough, she still had the same gentle smile and there was a special look in her eyes when hymns were being sung in the nursing home. She had always been a Christian and was a great woman for her church.

My father's life fell into a pattern. In the mornings, he would spend time gardening, visit one of the family who lived close for a light lunch or a cup of tea and he spent the afternoons at the nursing home. He hated the evenings, especially the long winter evenings, as he was lonely. Although most of his children lived close by, they spent time in the evenings with their own partners who had been working all day. We all visited dad as much as we could, but he felt it was never enough and he told us how lonely he was at every opportunity. Apart from the newspaper he didn't read anything else and we couldn't get him interested in television. My sister, who lived alone, started staying with him two or three nights a week. She worked during the day and had settled in her own little apartment so moving in permanently was never an option.

Having no woman for company got to my father. His health suffered, and, worryingly, he had started falling. When the GP examined him after a fall, she gave him a memory test. Soon after, he attended a specialist clinic for the diagnosis of Alzheimer's and dementia, and it was confirmed he had the latter. Next time he fell, he broke his collarbone. Convalescing in a nursing home after the fall, it was decided his mobility problem had left him incapable of living alone. After much discussion with the family he agreed to join his wife in the nursing home. It was just as well as he needed twenty-four hour care.

Now, the two of them sit side by side every day and the family visit on a regular basis. There are different types of dementia and thankfully he still knows us two years after being diagnosed. Each time the family visit he tells us he loves every one of us and it is wonderful to hear. We are his children and we tell him we love both him and our stepmother. All of this has been hard for the family, but we know that my father and stepmother are being taken good care of and that is the best we can hope for. As I write, my father is eighty-eight and his wife is eighty-four.

**

My mother's husband, John had been devoted to her care for years before she died. Shortly after, he found himself a girlfriend, much younger than himself and this did not go down well with some of the family. He passed away three years after my mother and I feel he was happy during that time.

Finding The Peace of
The Taj Mahal

Daniel and I had been through so much that we felt it would be good to downsize and move to a little bungalow beside the sea. We had been living in the bungalow in Larne that we purchased after coming home from Spain, it was quite big and the gardens took a lot of maintenance. I had always wanted a sea view and now it was time to buy something smaller.

Fate had other ideas; while looking for the little bungalow, we went to see the most beautiful five-bedroom house just a few miles along the coast. It had three bathrooms, two sitting rooms, a kitchen and a dining room. The large balcony had uninterrupted views across the sea to Scotland. There was a little recreation room with a bar and a boat came with the house as part of the deal.

We fell in love with the place. I imagined our children and grandchildren staying with us for holidays and the parties we would have. I could have Angel Awareness workshops and perhaps offer accommodation to people who needed a retreat while consciously following their Spiritual Path. There was a choice of hotels nearby, so I wouldn't have to cook dinner for them.

I felt I had it all worked out.

We put our own house up for sale and placed an offer on the dream house. We had quite a few viewers and one couple said they would buy it. Once again we filled a bedroom with packed boxes, the treasures of a lifetime, things we could not do without — or at least that is what we told ourselves.

The sale of our house fell through!

The buyers had their house valued and it wasn't worth as much as they expected, so they couldn't afford to buy ours. We were back to square one.

We had to clear the bedroom of all the boxes and put them in the garage. We restaged the room as a bedroom and accepted viewers once again. We had been trying all this time to close the deal on our intended home, but there had been many delays.

Finally, a year after we had put our house on the market, it sold, but the agents still could not close the deal on the other one. They told us it could be another six months before it would be available. We could have rented a house for that time but we felt we had been messed around too much.

We had viewed two other properties in the area and made an offer on one of them. After all the grief and loss we had suffered, I couldn't believe I'd had my heart broken this time by losing the house I had invested so much of my thoughts and dreams in. I loved that house and losing it caused me much self-pity and soul-searching. I was planning to do something good for others in God's name. I was planning to inform others about Angels. Why-oh-why did we not get that house? Had I not been good enough?

The new house sat a little bit further back from the sea, but it had sea views and a balcony to enjoy them. It was in a lovely community with a community hall offering all types of courses. There were hotels, a pub with live music and a shop close by. It was just a short walk to the bus stop, the children's play park and the beach. Family and friends were quick to point out that this house suited us better than the one I had wanted. It was a long time before I could talk about the other one without tears.

One evening we were driving past it to go to a concert in one of the local hotels, and as we were passing it I said to Daniel, "The house looks so dark and sad. I wish a wee family would come along to buy it and love it."

Not long after, I learned that someone had bought it for much less than we had offered for it. I felt glad that someone would be moving in. "If something is meant for you it will not go past you," so they say. Well, it wasn't meant for us no matter how much we wanted it, or how much we were pre-pared to pay.

I have had a lot of time to think about it, and I realise that as a healer, I had offered to serve God. Our neighbours have told us we have brought a bit of life to the area. Perhaps God wanted our healing energy to be exactly where it is at the moment.

Daniel has retired now and he seems happy. He once told me he could be happy anywhere and I know he was right. There was a lot of work to do to the new property to update it, and he is able to do most of it himself. It has kept him busy and that is how he likes to be. The house is big enough to have our children and grandchildren stay over, so they too are happy with it.

I have made friends in our neighbourhood. I have taken courses in Interior Design, Art and Creative Writing. I have been to a couple of Yoga classes and Daniel and I have made a point of going to musical evenings once a month in the hotel. We have not taken as many walks in our beautiful surroundings as we should have, but we can change that.

I now live beside the very same beach my grand-mother promised to take me to when I stayed with her as a little girl. When I walk beside it I feel her walking with me, in Spirit, her love and laughter given freely to me as she gave it to so many others in the past.

Daniel and I haven't been for any more of those adventurous holidays; nowadays we are happy to go to Spain to catch up with friends and we also holiday in Ireland, my father always said there was nowhere more beautiful when the sun shines and I think he was right.

My healing work has become more solitary. I have what the grandchildren call my Quiet Room. It is a sitting room with beautiful views of the garden. The room is cool in summer, but it has a log burning stove for cosy nights in winter. It has a calm, peaceful energy which everyone who enters comments on. There is a feeling of peace similar to the one I had at the Taj Mahal and maybe I had it in mind when we were decorating. The floor is a golden coloured wood while the walls, curtains and settees are cream. My healing bed and meditation chair are well placed to look out at nature. Bookcases hold my spiritual books, art equipment, music CDs and crystals.

When I escape to this room I play my music, light scented candles and I write, paint, read, think, pray and meditate. I read my Angel Cards and I send healing and love to those who need it. I also send it to the Earth, the Universe and the Universes beyond ours provided it is used for the highest and greatest good of all.

God has been good to me; I have much to be thankful for. When I count my blessings now, I count them twice. In return for all the love and support I have received from above I may yet write a book about my Spiritual Journey.

As a little girl going to that small country school I could never have envisaged what life held in store for me, the lovely family I would have, the people I would meet, the journeys I would make to all those wonderful countries. Most of all I never thought I would glimpse the next world from the one I am in at the moment.

I am still in touch with Kenny, the man who changed my life by telling me that I am a healer. I told him of my sadness when so many of the people of great wisdom left my life. He said that it is now my turn to be a woman of wisdom for others.

Is this the end of my story? I hope not. Daniel and I are both healthy, I am only sixty-five and Daniel is sixty-nine. We have been married for forty seven years. Life is what you make it and there are still adventures to be had, here on this beautiful Earth which we are privileged to be a part of.

Our youngest son asked us recently if we should be making a bucket list. We laughed at this, our life and travels developed without doing so in the beginning and we managed between us to see and experience quite a lot of the world. Having discussed it, we both feel that we have had a great life and although we are happy at home with the family at the moment, if something comes up that we fancy we will be off on our travels again.

I have been told that the Cherry Blossom in Japan is quite beautiful!

Acknowledgements

With thanks to the following people:

My husband, my lovely family and friends for their never ending support, love, patience and kindness.

Angeline King for inspiring my foray into creative writing, for her initial edit of the book and her continual friendship and support.

To Kenny Corris for introducing me to the gift of Healing and being an example of compassion for others and the Earth we inhabit.

My beautiful neighbour for being a listening ear for my work and encouraging me to keep writing. She knows who she is.

The Book Reality Experience for publishing my book and turning my dreams of being an author into a reality.

My Angels whose help and support was always available when I asked.

The Divine for giving me the privilege of spending time on this glorious Earth.

And finally, though by no means least, to you reader, for taking the time to read the story of my life. I thank you with all of my heart.

About The Author

Having discovered a love of writing in her sixties the author has had a couple of stories published in an anthology of Creative Writing.

Married with two sons, two wonderful daughters-in-law and five grandchildren, she has retired by the sea. Her passions are healing, writing, art, interior design and gardening. She also yearns for the next holiday to broaden her horizons and give her even more memories to include in her next book.

9 780648 949725